THE DRAFTNIK

A STORY ABOUT THE PRO FOOTBALL DRAFT
AND ITS IMPACT ON A DYSLECTIC

Drew Boylhart

iUniverse, Inc.
Bloomington

THE DRAFTNIK
A Story About The Pro Football Draft And Its Impact On A Dyslectic

iUniverse books may be ordered through booksellers or by contacting:

iUniverse
1663 Liberty Drive
Bloomington, IN 47403
www.iuniverse.com
1-800-Authors (1-800-288-4677)

ISBN: 978-1-4759-4417-4 (sc)
ISBN: 978-1-4759-4418-1 (ebk)

Printed in the United States of America

iUniverse rev. date: 08/08/2012

Dedication

This book is dedicated to my two sons Alex and Jonathan Boylhart who changed the true meaning of life for me and to Rob and Traci Esch who have tried to helped me in my struggles to become a better person but I don't think it's worked!

Introduction

The Shock was just too much. I could not believe what I just witnessed on TV. In the first round of the 2009 NFL draft the Buffalo Bills had just drafted Aaron Maybin DE/LB Penn St and I thought my head was going to fly off my body. This uncontrollable emotion was quickly followed with the throwing of my Froot Loops (milk and all) at the TV in a burst of anger. This selection in my opinion was a mistake of such magnitude that I just knew water boarding the person responsible (using the milk in my cereal bowl) would be acceptable!

For the reported forty million NFL draft fans who watch the draft on TV every year, the draft is not a hobby, a joke, or just a passing interest. The NFL Draft is a passion that allows us to escape from our real life worries and problems. Once a year the fans of the NFL are drawn into the life of a General Manager in a fantasy like status.

For me, it's a little more personal. The draft has affected my life more than most Draftniks I suspect. It helped me as a stress reliever, helped me to indentify my educational handicap (Dyslexia) and motivated me to overcome those handicaps cumulating into the writing this book. The draft also has given my sons and me something in common and a bond that no amount of time will be able to break.

Chapters

Chapter I

Becoming a Draftnik

How it all Started

My definition of a Draftnik is a person like myself: an overly confident, maniacal, annoying, arrogant human being with a little bit of OCD thrown in for good measure. Every Draftnik I know thinks they know everything about the draft and what we don't know we act like we do anyway. The natural Draftnik has one opinion and one opinion only about a player in the draft. We never admit we are wrong and feed off any information that pertains to the draft. We analyze everything because we believe everything has a meaning behind it. We also believe in football conspiracies. In short we are one loose screw away from having no screws and being completely nuts.

I ask myself all the time, how did this happen? How did this passion for the NFL draft take such an important place in my life? How does anyone go from doing anything in an unobtrusive way to having it take over his or her lives? Gradually I suspect, at least that's how my addiction to the NFL Draft happened for me. I had a small interest in the draft through the early years but it was never more than what most would consider a passing interest. Nevertheless, as we all know in life, a "passing interest" can turn into something much more and in this case it did just that.

As a former high school athlete my interest in sports never wavered after graduating but my ability to play competitive sports did. I did the normal adult beer league softball game thing, and played basketball at the YMCA but for me that wasn't enough. I did a walk on gig for a minor league baseball team and made the team but even that was short lived in spite of having good stats and being told all the time by the coaches that I was doing an excellent job. As all former athletes do who can't get enough mental or physical competitive stimulation, I started to look for just about anything sports related that would substitute.

At that time in the 70's the NFL draft was just starting to be talked about and reported on in magazines and newspaper but only after the draft was over. This made the draft an afterthought or just a passing interest for the average fan and it did just that for me also, that is until 1979 when the New York Giants drafted QB Phil Simms from Morehead State University with the seventh selection in the first round. I remember thinking . . . Morehead State? Where the hell is Morehead State University and, what in the world is a Morehead! At that time my father was a Giants fan therefore, I was a Giants fan and my interest in the draft was limited to just the Giants. Of course in later years that changed. In 1986 I moved to Buffalo New York and became proud fan of the Buffalo Bills. Let's get back to 1979.

In 1979, unlike professional sports in general, most college football games were not carried on network television and cable TV might have been in existence, but not as far as the average person was concerned. The exception was The University of Notre Dame Football and about four bowl games on New Year's Day. At that time, Notre Dame had a quarterback by the name of Joe Montana. I thought Joe would be an excellent player for an NFL team. In fact I thought he was the best quarterback in that draft. But of course without seeing any other quarterback available for the draft, how would I really know? But in my burgeoning Draftnik arrogance that did not mater, I saw Joe played and as far as I was concerned Joe was the best. That being said, the only thing I knew about Morehead State University was that they had never played Notre Dame! Hence my exasperation of the selection of a small school quarterback from an area of the country I never knew existed. After the selection of Phil Simms I found out very quickly that I was not the only one who had this shocked reaction. Needless to say, the New York Media was as shocked as I was and reacted quickly in a very negative way. This negative media reaction prompted the New York Giants to plant positive articles with friendly media on the "work behind the scenes" the Giants did before drafting Phil. This brought to my attention the use by the NFL of strategic marketing. This strategic marketing aspect intrigued me because it gave me more of a connection than just being a former athlete who studies players. It connected the competitive business man and former competitive athlete in me together and linked those two passions to the Draft.

Very shortly after that draft something happened that triggered the "Football Conspiracy" side of my natural Draftnik instincts. In spite of the positive public relation articles coming out of Giants headquarters there were also leaks to the press that Bill Walsh a well respected college coach, NFL position coach and 1979 Rookie Head Coach for the San Francisco 49er's had evaluated Phil and was interested in drafting him. According to reports back then and Phil Sims Wikipedia page now, just before the 1979 NFL Draft Bill Walsh flew to Morehead State with Assistant Coach Sam Wyche to work Simms out. Walsh was so impressed with Simms that he planned to draft him and preferred Phil over another young quarterback they scouted and worked out that being, Joe Montana. Here's the catch, Walsh might have wanted to draft Phil but as he said, not until the third round. We will never know who Walsh might have selected if both QB's were available at the same time but I think it is safe to suggest that Bill Walsh was not going to draft either of these two quarterbacks in the 1ˢᵗ round! This leak just stoked the fires for the New York Media and the fans of the New York Giants who already were dissatisfied over this selection.

In my mind, the thought process of rating and selecting any quarterback over Joe Montana was sacrilegious. I had watched Joe Montana and in my opinion, Joe Montana had no equal. Of course I based that opinion on some sort of fictional scouting because the truth was, because as I stated before, I had never paid attention or can remember ever seeing any other quarterbacks eligible for that draft. All I knew was that Joe Montana played for Notre Dame and all I ever saw was Notre Dame Football games. It seemed only logical to me that Joe was the very best quarterback in the 1979 draft! It didn't matter to me that Jack Thompson QB Washington St was considered by the experts as the best quarterback in the draft that year and in fact was the first quarterback drafted. In my arrogant, immature football talent evaluating mind I was thinking, how on earth could Thompson or Simms be better than Joe! Neither of them had ever played for Notre Dame! There you have it, the natural arrogance of that perplexing animal called the Draftnik.

This selection of Phil Simms by the Giants caught my interest in such a way that I started to follow his career and let me tell you, his career at the NFL level had as many ups and downs as an elevator in a woman's two-story shoe store.

Looking back on it now I realize this selection of a small college player so early in the draft triggered my stepping through the proverbial looking glass into the schizophrenic Draftnik world.

As you might have guessed, after that 1979 Draft, I started to study the draft a little more closely because the challenge was on. I had to know in my mind if I was right about Phil Simms and Joe Montana. I had to find away to get more information on the players available for the draft, before the draft. This crap about what happened after a team drafted a player was not working for me. I suspected much bull shit and I needed to know if I was right or wrong. So I started to hunt out any information on college players and this led me to finding and buying Joel Buchsbaum's Pro Football Draft Book. I bought this book for one reason, its size made it easy to hide. For some reason I felt shame with this uncontrollable, slow progression of compulsiveness that I was developing for the NFL Draft. Buchsbaum's book was erotic, pure eye candy, sports porno. Why did I have such shame over researching hard-core statistics? I don't know but for some reason I felt it would be embarrassing to be exposed. I guess it's possible the shame came from the fact that for the first time in my life this newfound passion was not within my control and evoking uncontrollable actions, like throwing the bowl of cereal at the TV. I had always been a person who kept his emotions under control publically, but this new passion was uncontrollable and addicting. This book was slowly bringing out in me all the feelings I suspected that nerds have when they engulf themselves in projects far beyond the ability of average human beings.

Buchsbaum's book was a human database of information on college prospects and often looked at some of the most obscure college teams. It had this enormous amount of information about the draft and still it was small enough to hide. Looking back on it now, I can see how my strange behavior about the NFL Draft might draw the same parallels to a husband carrying out an affair. This NFL Draft Guide was becoming my "mistress" and as my obsession grew like most mistresses, it started slowly to control me, seduce me, and eventually I feared, would make conflicting demands on my time.

The urge for information was so addicting that in the middle of the day I would hear or see a name of a player eligible for the upcoming draft in the newspaper or hear it on TV and scurry to my hiding place like a squirrel going to hide a walnut but instead I would do it to look at "the book". I would carefully turn each page slowly looking for all the information on that player. I needed to know where that player was rated in the top 100 or I could not sleep. I needed to know the details of his physical being, height, weight, age. I needed to know how fast he was. I was also, looking for what round that player might be selected in, and if the player might be available for my favorite team to draft. My obsessive behavior was becoming so out of control that I imagined that the book spoke to me and was secretly providing clues for me to read between the lines and form new predictions. I felt like I had begun to understand Joel Buchsbaum's obsessive mind. I was sure that I had pierced the veil of Buchsbaum's subtle writing signals of who he thought was a good player and who was just an average player. I knew this because the book spoke to me and me alone . . . or so I thought!

I never spoke to anyone about my interest in the draft in those early years because I thought people would call me a nut or worse . . . a nerd! You have to understand, I believed my interest in the draft was not for "cool guys" like me. After all, I was a former High School top athlete who dated the head cheerleader, the best dancer, and lead singer of a high school rock and roll band. I was hot stuff . . . or so I thought!

Where I did not succeed was academics and this subconsciously, might have been the real reason for hiding my interest in the draft. For me, college, academically and financially was not an option. Knowing this at an early age made high school of less importance to me. The truth is I thought I was dumb because I could not pass a simple test.

Later in life I did take a few verbal IQ tests at a local University and was told at times I scored as high as 160 on some of them but in high school I was severely handicapped when it came to taking a simple test or regent's exam. In the small town high school I graduated from, the teachers gave me a pass. I suspect they were tired of my class clown ways and having to deal with my disruptive wit. My lack of interest in education in general, made this draft thing more intellectual and required more reading then I had ever done in my life. As you might have guessed by now, reading a book was like reading a foreign language to me. Oh I read very well I just could not understand what I was reading. I learned by touching, doing, listening and using selective memory. I listened to how people talked and used words in sentences to establish a vocabulary that made people think I was educated but the truth is I really didn't know what most of the words I used meant. I just used them the same way others did in a sentence to cover for my lack of a true education. I don't remember ever opening up a book in High School! Being part of a family of seven other siblings I either played on sports teams or worked after school. I didn't have time for books. As far as I was concerned, I passed my courses without reading a book so what was the big deal? Or so I thought!

The draft changed all of that for me. I'm embarrassed to admit that it made me open up the first book I can ever remember reading. Nevertheless, it did and the truth is I think that embarrassment was the real reason behind my covert behavior about the draft all along. I really thought for some stupid reason that people would just think I attained all of this information through osmoses. After all, if they knew differently it would mess with my reputation. Or so I thought! In later years I discovered that I was and am dyslectic but it took until this writing to admit that to myself and I don't mind telling you it's a little scary. I was never told that I was dumb but I was told that I was lazy all my life. I realize now that I was able to fool everybody about this lack of ability to learn because I developed other skills to compensate.

Not unlike I suppose, a left handed person has to compensate and adapt to living in a right handed world. These learned skills that I developed to hide and compensate are the skills that I use now to profile players for the draft and the skills I used as a business man to survive, compete and succeed. So I guess it isn't really that much of a problem once it is identified but that is the key, to indentify it early.

Life continued typically, as it would for any young man, work, marriage, starting a family. All of this left less time for interests in hobbies and studying the draft took a back seat on the priority meter. Nevertheless, the draft was always simmering below the surface waiting to come to a full boil at any time. As the years went on and the general pressure of everyday married life started to catch up to me, I looked for a distraction and in doing so, the seductive whispering in my head started to get louder.

It's not unusual, for people to turn to alcohol, drugs, extramarital affairs, or gambling to manage stress. Some men go out to the garage, or hang out in the local hardware store. Some go on long fishing trips or hunting trips or play golf or run marathons, anything to stop their minds from thinking about their problems. I was too tired and didn't have the money for drinking, gambling, or drugs. I didn't have a garage and the local hardware stores were full of old guys who were looking at power tools with more drool and emotion than they looked at their wives. That was just damn scary to me. For me there was nothing left to do but give in to my mistress so, I turn to the draft. Little did I know the future impact it would have on my life!

In spite of my success in using the draft as a stress reliever, it was taking me away from interacting with my family. To address this problem and in an effort to interact more with my sons, I mentioned the draft to them and bought a different Draft magazine the day before the 1994 draft. I remember sitting in the parking lot of the local super market talking to my eight year old son and asking him who he thought the Buffalo Bills were going to draft. Now remember, the only college football that we saw with regularity still at this time was the Notre Dame games so it makes sense that my son would pick the highly rated Jeff Burris CB who played for; you guessed it, Notre Dame. The next day we listened to the draft on the radio and low and behold, the Buffalo Bills did select Jeff Burris in the first round. We danced as if we had just won the Lottery for a million dollars. For me the passion was back but for my sons it started their passion for the draft that continues to this day.

The joy of discovering other potential Draftniks (my sons) had started me down the path of coming out of the Draftnik closet. I had stumbled on a new and more semi public hiding place for my passion. I could hide my passion for the draft in my eight year old son and my other son who at the time was four years old and no one would be the wiser.

I was now free to buy as many draft books and magazines as I wanted because I could now justify buying those periodicals using the excuse that the reason for buying them was because of my deep devotion to my sons and their passion for the draft. I know pretty pathetic! Nevertheless, using my poor unsuspecting sons as a foil, gave me the freedom to engage in endless discussion about the draft and no one would be the wiser. That is as long as one of my sons was in the room with me! Of course, if only my four year old son was in the room the poor little chipmunk had no idea what I was talking about. Eventually, the boys and I started having dinner in front of the TV during draft season and when any draft news came on, I made sure the ice cream came out to keep them focused and in front of the TV. After all, I had a responsibility to educate my sons on the NFL draft, right!

In spite of involving my sons, I still continued to be embarrassed and held back on letting any close friends or relatives know of my true passion for the draft. After all I was a grown man, with two children and a business owner. I was convinced the draft was for young kids who couldn't get a date and who played on those silly new things called computers. A few years later after surviving a divorce, selling my business, becoming a single parent, and starting a new job, the stress made my daily life at times unbearable. Through it all, three things gave me structure and the ability to navigate through the tough times, my two sons, and my loyal mistress . . . The Draft.

Starting that new job became the surprise benefit of all the new changes in my life. Running my own business for ten years was a 365 day a year job with no holidays or weekends off. My new 8 am to 5 pm job in state government with weekends and holidays off helped me define and understand better the politics of the draft. This new job also gave me another benefit that up until now eluded me and stunted my growth as a Draftnik. For the first time in years, I had a job that gave me the weekends off. Do you understand what that meant? Having the weekends off meant I could WATCH the draft on TV! I was now free to become an official draft nerd or as I like to say an official Draftnik.

The NFL Draft on TV was truly the first reality show. It was live and unscripted, like a reality show is suppose to be. It is also boring yet at the same time strangely addicting. At least for me it is!

It's addicting because every pick is an emotion that comes in waves and leaves you waiting and wanting more. Now that I think about it in comparison it's similar to sex, interesting! The draw of NFL Draft, mock drafts, top 100 list and studying athletes available for the draft, goes beyond social networking and competition. It is not simply trying to guess the player or players our teams want to add to their roster. We Draftniks want to be a part of a team's building success. I'm not sure why, maybe it's because we struggle for emotional control in our personal lives. On the other hand, maybe it's just for the simple enjoyment of a guilt free fantasy! This fantasy aspect of the draft has always intrigued me and has been studied for centuries.

Sigmund Freud believed that the average person could not exist without daydreams. That being said, I didn't become a Draftnik because I wanted to. I became a Draftnik because I needed to. At least for me, looking back at the slow process of how this obsession took control of my life—that's how I see it!

Chapter II

Joining A Draft Site

The Huddle Report.com

In 2002, when we all discovered that Al Gore had invented the Internet, I was working at a state agency that had begun to use the Internet to support its public education and research efforts. In the office, my internet access was limited to work related web searches, but I was slowly beginning to sense there was more. At this point, I was still getting all my draft information and stats from television, magazines and newspapers but I was becoming curious about draft information that was becoming available through the Internet. Still, if it wasn't for my two sons I'm not sure I would have bought a personal computer! I was satisfied with having access to a computer at work. My two sons campaigned for a home computer using the lame excuse of "how could they possibly succeed in school without one"! I actually fell for that crap and bought one. Good thing!

Personal Internet access was a game changer. A new frontier was open to me. With my son's guidance, I stumbled on all this new draft information on the internet that I never knew existed. It seems my mistress (the Draft) had "gone viral" and I was very happy and doing the dance of joy. The draft had made me open up a book for the first time in my life and now it had motivated me to educate myself using a computer and discover a new world of knowledge that I never knew existed. The benefit out of all of this was that it could be done in the secrecy of my home and I could continue my covert draft life, the closet was still closed. Whew!

In my quest for draft information and stats, I found myself a frequent visitor of a website called, "The Huddle Report. com." I used this site and a number of other sites to find information on player profiles, stats, and draft boards. The most valuable tool on THR for me was the value board that showed you what round a player might be selected in with excellent accuracy.

I had learned a long time ago that while I had a consistent record in assessing a player's ability to be successful in the NFL I lacked the skill to predict which round that player might be selected. I can remember listening to the draft year after year and wondering why a player who I suspected was going to be an excellent player would not be selected until sometimes as late as the 4th and 5th rounds of a draft and sometimes not drafted at all. In discovering The Huddle Report.com, I now had a tool for determining what round a player I liked, might be drafted in. The funny thing about this discovery was even if a player who I thought was going to be excellent was listed on THR founder Rob Esch's value board as a 5th or 6th rounder, it did not change my personal profile of that player's ability to impact. I just thought whoever selects that player is going to get a hell of a football player late in the draft. Unwittingly that thinking was a prelude to the two board system we use now on the site but at that time, it was just the pure arrogance of a Draftnik.

Sometime in the 2003 draft season, a profile about Terrell Suggs DE/OLB Arizona St, appeared on The Huddle Report.com that I thought was nuts. I decided for the first time in my life to e-mail this profiler and tell him why I thought he was wrong about Terrell.

This was big for me because at that time my typing skills were rudimentary at best and as far as I was concerned, Al Gore had made one big mistake, spell check was not on most computers for e-mail. Teaching myself how to type, forced me to spell check every e-mail I wrote on word perfect first, and then copy and paste it to the outgoing e-mail box. My spelling was so bad at that time that spell check would crash, that is until it developed a message stating it had "no suggestions" for the word I was trying to spell. I'm the type of person who could figure out the most complex problems, socially, politically and for any type of business successfully. I could look at a profit and loss statement and tell you why and where you are losing money without walking into your business. At the same time, I struggled to add a simple column of numbers but understood algebra and geometry without looking at a book. I never seem to have a problem reading sentences but understanding what I just read had always been a problem for me. As the years went on I did a good job of teaching myself how to understand what I was reading by reading every other word in a sentence instead of every word to get the idea behind the sentence, and then reading the sentence as a whole to understand it.

Reading this way became easy and automatic and because I didn't know any better, I just thought everyone read that way. Nevertheless reading for me was time consuming and because of this I didn't have the patience to read a whole book. Furthermore, taking a test was almost impossible because of the time constraints. I have failed just about every written test I have ever taken. When I was young I thought this was because I was stupid and I hid the fact that I didn't understand what I was reading by reading with a flair for the dramatics and with inflictions and facial expressions that would make people laugh to take attention away from my struggles. I became the class clown to hide the fact that I was what we have identified know as Dyslectic. The truth is my interest in the draft motivated me to read sport magazines and the sport sections of the newspapers. Of course none of that happened until I was out of High School. In school the teachers all loved me because I was quick witted, smart acting, had all the answers, when asked. At the same time they all considered me lazy, careless, immature, a dreamer, hard to control, and in general a comedic disruptive pain in the ass. They got mad at me because my test scores were poor and because when they asked me the questions, I knew the answer. They were very frustrated with me and me with them. Being interested in the draft and having spell check on the computer slowly helped me to become productive and allowed me to have the confidence in the future to write profiles. Of course all of that didn't happen until I was in my 50's. I still type words that I think are correct but when I go to check the spelling of those words, up comes that squiggly line under the word telling me I'm wrong. As word perfect improved and it included the ability to research words after they were spelled correctly I learned I had mistakenly acquired a pretty good vocabulary memorizing and remember how a word was used in a sentence. This was my first inclination that I had a problem. I knew how to use words but I didn't know how to spell them. In my mind that was convoluted. But in my defense, before spell check I was not able to look a word up in a dictionary because I didn't know how to spell it. The strange thing about being dyslectic for me was, as I stated before, I believe it had a collateral advantage. I think it forced me to develop other skills that might have laid dormant in me.

Getting back to the profile of Terrell Suggs, this particular profiler suggested that Terrell was a "tweener defensive end/outside linebacker" and would most likely have little impact in the NFL. At this time in the NFL most teams were not using the 3/4 style of defense that Terrell might excel in. Most teams were using the traditional 4/3 defense that required four big down lineman.

I suspect for this reason most scouts would consider Terrell too small to be a defensive end in a 4/3 defense and too large or not athletic enough to be a linebacker in a 3/4 defense, hence the dreaded label of "tweener".

The "tweener" label is the kiss of death for a defensive player and that is not what I saw on the field when I looked at Terrell. What I saw was special instincts in how Terrell played and I saw those instincts on display in Holiday Bowl against Kansas St. Terrell showed leadership skills along with those excellent instincts in a losing cause. He never stopped working and had a total of four solo tackles, two for loses along with two sacks. He was a monster and the one player Kansas St had to play away from all game long.

After reading the profile on Suggs that predicted he would have little impact in the NFL, and labeling him a "tweener" my profiling instincts and emotions went into the kind of shock that incapacitated me for a moment like an ice cream headache. I knew differently about this kid and in a strongly, yet professionally worded e-mail to the profiler, I stated my case. As far as I was concerned he simply missed the boat with Terrell. Not only did I believe Terrell would impact in any style of defense but Terrell reminded me (in his play on the field) of a former NFL player Charles Haley DE/LB San Francisco 49er's. I could not understand how anybody could suggest that this pass rushing, tackling machine was going to be ordinary at the next level! I created the e-mail, banging away on my computer in complete exasperation, and in spite of spell check begging to commit suicide; I sent it and forgot about it.

The most satisfying feeling happened to me on the day of the 2003 draft, Terrell was drafted in the 1st round by the Baltimore Ravens and selected as the tenth best player in that draft. I felt a surge of justification about that e-mail I had sent. At the time little did I realize there was something else that e-mail did for me. Unbeknownst to me, I had mistakenly broken into the world of public profiling.

At some point after that draft I received an email from Robby Esch at The Huddle Report.Com. It seems that Rob and this particular profiler had parted ways. In cleaning up some old work, Rob had read my e-mail and wanted to know if I wanted to do profiles for the site. I thought it was a joke.

The truth is, I felt I wasn't qualified to do something like that. Oh, I had no doubts about my ability to profile a player, that wasn't the issue. Every job I have ever had required me to quickly profile people. That ability along with being a former athlete and developing business survival skills, predicated on a highly developed sense of observational instincts, made me confident in my ability to create a profile. The catch for me was, I didn't think I was qualified because I could not spell, never read a book and had limited education. The truth is, I thought Rob was nuts to even ask me but Rob had instincts also and his instincts told him I might be good at writing profiles. My sons were very excited and took turns talking me into it. Both of my sons told me that I was doing the work anyway so why not write down my thoughts on a player for everybody to see. After all what did I have to lose? Pride? Dignity? No, I had misplaced those a long time ago.

After a great deal of self debate, I decided that if I was going to do this, I wasn't going to produce profiles like everyone else did. I didn't want to create a profile that did not give a reason why a player was going to be successful or not successful at the next level. I wanted to do profiles based on the facts, but also profiles that included my intuition, instincts, and the talent I had developed over the years to "read people". I personally do not consider these skills I have learned over the years as anything special. In fact this talent of "reading people" developed over the years from my life experiences, is a talent that I knew many people had developed and used in their everyday lives attained through there own life experiences. I believed incorporating these "reading people" skills would make my profiles more identifiable and entertaining. I also felt it would set me apart from others who were doing profiles for the public at that time. I wanted to do profiles that showed the passion that a fan has for the sport. I knew that playing football at the NFL level took more than athletic talent and that reporting just how many tackles a talented college player made was a small part of profiling a player. As far as I was concerned, the real key to profiling a player was *how* they played the game. So, I e-mailed Rob back, gave him my phone number, and we talked. We both seemed to be on the same page about how the profiles should be written and agreed that these profiles should be written like a group of guys getting together, having some beers, and just talking. We both knew that for the average fan, telling them that a player has great hand usage or runs great routes is helpful but is not the information a fan really wants to know on draft day. When it is all said and done, fans really want to know how good or bad a player might be and what round he will be drafted in.

To keep the profiles unique, I wanted to use simple language that everyone could understand and stay away from professional "scout" talk. My professional background has its base in business management and that was something unique that I could bring to the profiling process along with seeing the impact of a player to a franchise through the eyes of an owner. I thought maybe there were business people, and professionals interested in the draft as a stress reliever like me, and they would appreciate this new point of view. To accomplish this new style of profiling I would include along with the normal evaluation of athletic talents, character, football intelligence and instincts. I would also add marketability and my favorite aspect of drafting a player, length till impact or "LTI" as I like to call it. I knew profiling a player using these guidelines would be very different and unique and set me aside from others who try to profile players for the public.

In doing public profiles I knew there would be one issue that would come up and I mentioned that to Rob on the first day. Because I have an opinion about a player and write a public profile that does not make me a scout. That would be an insult to the hard working scouts in the business for years. I have an opinion and that opinion may at times agree with a scout's opinion but that does not make me a scout. I'm a profiler who analyses people to give you a snap shot into their potential to succeed. I do not interview players or see them live or collect information on a player's personal background. I do not travel all over the United States missing family holidays & birthdays and living out of motels and eating food that might put me in a hospital. In Joining THR I wanted to drive the point home to everyone who loved the draft as I do, that I held the ultimate credential for the job of Draftnik. I am a self educated football fan. I have watched, coached, played, lived and at times felt like I was going to die for the sport of football for over 30 years and those are my qualifications for profiling players for the draft, but I'm not a scout, I'm not that good.

Rob and I knew it would take time to educate the average fan who had gotten use to a certain style of profile to accept something that was new and different. Nevertheless, I knew I could indentify talent and potential. I also knew I could read people and produce a solid profile.

I knew all of this because like many other people, I had been doing it all my life. After disusing this with Rob and feeling we were both on the same page, I officially joined "The Huddle Report.com" for the 2004 draft season.

Chapter III

Sports Illustrated Interview

Coming Out of the Draftnik Closet

The B S Detector

After the first year of doing profiles, Rob and I decided that we had to do something to gain more control over the site. All the e-mails and radio shows and interviews had gotten a little out of hand along with announcers on TV and Radio using information from the profiles. Rob and I had no problem with people using information from his value board and Mock Draft contest and Top 100 board contest or the profiles. What we both had a problem with was not getting credit for it. I mean seriously, if you are going to tell me I'm an "amateur" and then turn around and use my information to form your "expert" opinion, don't you think that's the same thing as stealing proprietary information? All Rob and I ever asked for was credit for our hard work, is that too much to ask for? Rob and I agreed that if the experts were going to use our information and not give us credit for it, we could at least get some money from them. At this point, the decision was to make The Huddle Report.com a membership site at a price that most people could afford. It wasn't until the site became a membership site did we realize how much the media and the networks were using our information. We also realized at that point, how many executives and people in all different professional fields enjoyed the site. It was a revelation and I started to feel that maybe I was not alone. Maybe the NFL draft's true marketing niche was not just 20 year old nerds, who in truth I was of kindred spirit with.

In 2008, in spite of the site being a membership site for three years, the fact that the media knew about us was obvious when Selena Roberts of Sports Illustrated contacted Rob. I'm not sure how Selena knew about us because I didn't envision her being a Draftnik but she did find us and for some reason she decided to do an article on the draft using us. Rob was excited, gave Selena my name, and called me to tell me that Selena would be contacting me for an interview after she interviewed him.

At that time, I had dealings with the media when I worked for the Governor of New York State as a Special Assistant. That being said, I was naturally suspicious of the media. In fact, my first reaction about this interview was negative. Being a former appointee, I suspected this might be a back door way to try and embarrass the former governor, who at that time had thoughts of running in the next presidential election. Now I seriously understand how crazy that sounds to most of you but for those of you who have worked in the world of politics, I'm sure you can identify with this thought process. The media is well known in political circles for writing articles with a negative motivation behind them but this was not the only reason for my suspicious and paranoid behavior. Remember for years, my peers at work, my friends and even my siblings, had no real knowledge of the extent of my involvement and passion for the draft. I might have talked about the draft but only in passing and as it involved my two sons. I would never even suggest to anyone that I stayed up nights looking at film and writing profiles. I was still in the Draftnik closet and using my two sons to hide the extent of the affair with my mistress (The Draft). Doing an interview would bring me out of the closet to everyone. I mean we are talking about freaking Sports Illustrated! Not some small local paper or a radio show that most of my friends and siblings, had no idea existed. This was a mainstream sports media magazine that reached almost every house and bathroom in America! Rob was excited but I never let on until this writing that I was conflicted, anxious, and so upset that I thought for sure, for me bowel movements would become a thing of the past. Rob told me that Selena was going to contact me in a few days to interview me and that did it for me. I went right to the computer and did a search on Selena Roberts and guess what I found, I found what I thought would be the enemy! I found out that Selena had previously worked for the New York Times, the mother of all enemies for a registered Republican. For those of you who don't follow politics The New York Times has a habit of not being very favorable to anybody who holds political office, especially if you are a republican. At least that was the consensus in my political world. I think you can guess what my next reaction was. I thought for sure this was going to be a set up and how would I ever explain to Rob that we should not do this interview.

Rob lived in Texas and was so removed from New York politics that trying to make him understand that this interview could be a set up to embarrass a former Governor who was thinking of running for the top office in the country was just going to be impossible. I had visions of the article coming out that attacked me as an appointed Special Assistant who worked for the Governor of New York and who looked at film and did profiles on state time. That never happened because I was always worried that exact situation could happen and blow up in my face. Besides, I was one state employee that worked his ass off and was proud of it. I have never done a job half assed and was not about to be accused of that now. Nevertheless, that doesn't matter to the media when they decide to go after a politician. They will spin a story to imply anything they want with little repercussions for telling the truth. This was a disaster waiting to happen and I was just beside myself.

Now Selena Roberts did not deserve this paranoid reaction by me at all. Selena was an accomplished sports writer. According to her Bio on the NY Times web site, prior to joining The NY Times, Selena had served as the Minnesota Vikings beat writer at The Minneapolis Star Tribune. Before that, she worked as the Orlando Magic beat writer at the Orlando Sentinel from July 1993 to August 1994. Prior to that as the Tampa Bay Buccaneers beat writer from July 1992 to July 1993, including coverage of the N.F.L. playoffs and Super Bowl. Her resume also includes motorsports as the Volusia County beat writer from August 1991 to July 1992, covering NASCAR, and IMSA events, including the Daytona 500 and 24 hours of Sebring. This is just part of this woman's accomplishments and proof to any sane person that Selena was an accomplished sports writer now writing for Sports Illustrated and did nothing to deserve this type of reaction by me. Of course, you realize I said any sane person, and I never said I was sane! In my paranoid schizophrenic world I struggled understanding why Selena would think to do an article about me or The Huddle Report com. On its face it was difficult for me to get my head around and I had no choice but to think that this woman must be up to something because all I saw in her extensive resume was NEW YORK TIMES! Added to that was the fact that I also saw a woman sportswriter who was way out of my league as a professional writer.

I had a couple of days before the interview, and all I did was worry about what I would say and try be ready for any questions that might be asked of me about working for the governor. Seriously, all I needed in my life was the Attorney General's Office of New York involving me in an investigation that might embarrass the Governor.

In working for the Governor I had taught myself how to handle the media and stay under the media radar. I learned to stay under the media radar so well my co workers started to call me "stealth". My fear now was because of this interview that was about to change. I felt like I was right in the media's crosshairs. I was going crazy and the only thing I knew to calm myself down was to go back to looking at film and doing profiles. That has always been the calming factor in my life in times of stress and believe me this was a time of stress.

The day finally came and Selena was excellent to work with. In the first two minutes of the conversation, I knew I was working with a professional. The real surprise for me was Selena was truly only interested in doing an article about the draft and the quirky Draftnik community. This interview had nothing to do with my former position. In fact, she didn't even know that I had worked for the Governor, (Stealth Baby, Stealth) Once I got comfortable I opened up and told her things that I was surprised came out of me. It was like an intervention of some sort. I guess subconsciously I decided to come out of that Draftnik closet. The interview did not last that long and I figured after the initial contact that everything was over. I figured, Selena had her information and I was in the clear. Boy was I ever wrong about that because a funny thing happened on draft day.

In 2008, draft days were two day marathons. I would get up in the morning of the draft after about two hours of sleep and try to keep myself busy until the draft would start. It was excruciating because I got up at 6:00 am and the draft in those days did not start until I think about noontime. The truth is it's all a bit of a haze. I would cook food to last for two days for the boys so I didn't have to turn away for any length of time from the TV and miss a selection. Before the draft started, I would do work around the house to try to calm down.

Being a single parent I did all of the encompassing things around the house that only housewives can appreciate. I would do the wash, mow the lawn, vacuum the house, and one year I even changed the oil in my car. The problem with that is I got so wacked out that I had started something that I might not finish (before the draft started) that I left the car without the oil plug and new oil until I could get back to it after the draft was over, two days later. To try to explain to you the depth of my fanatical behavior for the draft I could not take a shower after the first day if my team made some very good selections because it might wash off the good luck! That goes for wearing and sleeping in the same clothes for the two days. I trained the boys at a young age to accept this type of behavior because it was a special occasion. You have to understand, to an adult Draftnik, there is no other day that comes close to giving you that same feeling that you had when you were a kid, of waking up on Christmas morning to those beautifully wrapped presents under the tree. I not only got up at 6:00 AM in the morning but I was so excited I'd wake the boys up at 6:00 AM too, and do a conga line down the stairs singing, "It's draft day, it's draft day, dada—dada—dada—da. The boys when they were younger thought this type of behavior was neat and later as they got older they thought everyone in the world did these strange rituals. They considered the draft a national holiday and thought this was normal behavior. I'm not sure it has dawn on them to this day that it's not. I do know they realize that their father might have a screw or two loose but as far as draft day and my behavior, in their opinion my behavior on that day was normal.

Now my memory is a little shaky as to what exactly happened next but I do remember that on the second day of the draft the phone rang. While the draft is in progress, at that time, I did not answer the phone, do interviews, or answer e-mails. Of course that behavior has changed now but back then, as far as I was concerned, the draft was too important. I did nothing that might take my attention away from the TV and the possibility of missing a selection. In my crazed Draftnik haze, I felt some sort of strange obligation to keep track and critic every pick and decide for myself if a team had made a good selection. I know pathetic, what can I say! On draft weekend I would tell everyone in my family and from work that I would be away for the weekend with my sons and not to call my cell because I just wanted some private time with my boys. Being a single parent everyone respected that and no one would call on draft weekend.

You have to remember I was still in the Draftnik closet and telling anyone the truth just was not going to happen. Using my sons as foil was just part of the draft process and looking back at it now I still don't feel bad. I should but I don't!

Since I had a no phone call policy for that weekend every year you can imagine my surprise when all of a sudden in the middle of the draft my home phone rings. I was very tempted not to answer it and let it go to voice mail but I thought that it could be an emergency. With massive doubt of this phone calls possible importance, I decided to answer the phone screaming the word "Crap" at the top of my lungs just before I picked it up. Surprise, it was Selena wanting to do a follow up for the article.

Now I really liked Selena, and she was very nice and I bet most of you would think how exciting this was, Sports Illustrated is calling, and . . . it's a woman too! Not me, not pathetic Drew! No, my first thought was, "Doesn't this woman know its draft day!!! Is she nuts! Doesn't she know that you can call me on Christmas morning while my sons are opening up their presents but you don't call me on draft day? Good thing for me my "dealing with the media" instincts kicked in and I was polite when she asked, "Can I get some of your reactions and feelings right now about what has happened so far in the draft"? Crap, this was going to be long. It might last two selections or more and they happen every five minutes! This woman must be nuts! I quickly turned back to the TV because I thought I might miss a selection and started to spew with excitement and at the same time showered her with the frustration that every Draftnik has while the draft is going on. I could not control what was coming out of my mouth. I was so excited that I knew I must have sounded like an Amish teenager during Rumspringa visiting his first stripper club. The floodgates opened and Selena used most of what I said in her article. I got off the phone and thought for sure that I was screwed. Nevertheless, in spite of feeling like I had just been screwed by a national magazine, I had more important things to attend to, the start of the seventh round! As the seventh round was going on, the Green Bay Packers were on the clock and proceeded to selected Matt Flynn QB LSU. I knew this team was going to be a hell of a team in a few years.

This kid was the real deal and along with Aaron Rodgers, I knew this team was set at the QB position to make a run for the Super Bowl in a few years. Later in the seventh round, the Broncos selected Peyton Hills RB Arkansas another player I considered "steal" material. I was on cloud nine big time. I had a lot invested in both of those player's profiles and knew that I was on the credibility clock for the next three years with the Draftnik world.

After the article came out a tsunami hit the Boylhart e-mail box and I loved it. People I haven't heard from in years contacted me to congratulate me and talk to me about the draft. Selena's article had made me feel that there was no longer a need to hide my affair with the draft. People thought it was cool that I wrote profiles and did radio interviews. Selena's article set me free and "Stealth" was no longer my moniker. I was now "The B S Detector" of The NFL Draft because I understood how to cut through all the crap. That's what Selena crowned me as in her article and I knew it fit me like a glove. Selena was one media person who had no hidden agenda to interview me, and just wanted to give a quirky unknown Draftnik some acknowledgment for his hard work. Nevertheless, my paranoid feelings about being interviewed for the article were not totally without merit.

After the article came out a person (who I knew of, but who did not know me), decided to call Selena and attack her about me. You see, in politics it works both ways. No matter what you think about the press, or party you may have an affiliation with, all sides know how to work the system in a negative way to try to take advantage and payback is the main goal of all parties. I knew Selena had an incident in her past with some articles where politics reared its ugly head and hung her out. I suspect this was more of an attack on Selena then it was on me. Nevertheless, this person called Selena and challenged her on the facts of my working for the Governor. I could only imagine how upset Selena might have been at the time. I mean seriously, all she did, was a simple puff piece article about the NFL Draft and a quirky Draftnik and she gets attacked and accused of possibly misrepresenting facts. Someone from Sports Illustrated called me right away and asked me how they could verify that I had worked for the Governor. I anticipated something like this was going to happen so I was prepared and gave them the telephone number of the office of appointees for the Governor. Sports Illustrated verified that I did indeed work for the Governor for over nine years. That's politics, there is always somebody out there trying to take you down and now you might understand better why the media acts the way it does sometimes. They are attacked as much as they attack. For those of you who have not seen the article written by Selena it's on the site and also part of Sports Illustrated public archives.

Chapter IV

Draftnik Training Camp

So, you want to be a Draftnik? Most of you already are just on different levels. The young draftniks are interested in a possible career in the media or becoming scouts for an NFL franchise. They are obsessed with collecting other people's information, talking "scouts speak" and lack a definite direction for their goals. The middle aged Draftnik is looking for stress relief that has no monetary affect on the family budget. They are interested in any information that will take their minds off their problems. The older Draftnik like me struggles with the ineptness of some NFL franchises when it comes to one of the most important aspects of developing a successful business, the hiring of talented people to run that business in this case the draft. We older Draftniks are people who have or had enormous responsibilities in our business lives and cannot believe it is as hard as most insist it is to evaluate talent for the NFL draft. We are not out to prove anyone else is wrong, just to prove ourselves right.

Have you heard the expression that profiling player for the NFL is not a science? That's because I believe it's not just about measurements and workouts. It's not about being black or white or if a person believes in religion or not and it's not about who is fat or skinny or tall or short.

In fact, if you have a negative personality, or are prejudice in any way, you will NOT be a good profiler. The best profilers I know are the most non-discriminating people. The worst profiler, are people who think profiling is a form of discrimination and use it that way.

Webster's definition of the word discriminate is,—the <u>unfair treatment</u> of one person or group, usually because of <u>prejudice</u> about a race, ethnicity, age, religion, or gender.

Webster's definition of the word profile is,—a brief description that summarizes the characteristics of somebody or something.

Politics in this country has made the word "profile" or a person who profiles, falsely interpreted to mean, a person who discriminates, but in truth, it is only a person who indentifies characteristics of other people for the ability to interact with them. In business, profiling is a survival technique and an important skill that is needed to be successful in negotiations.

When I joined THR my earlier conversations with Robby Esch revealed a mutual respect for the power of "profiling by film". There was only one way for us to get film on college players at that point and that was by taping the games ourselves as they originally aired on TV. We started the process with VCR's and volume, taping as many games as we could. I had six VCR's connected to one television taping games on different channels and Rob had just as many at his house. In an effort not to miss a single play, I simultaneously viewed as many live games as I could, not wanting to miss any action. Taping games allowed me to look at a player individually when I profiled him for talent and techniques. However, watching the game gave me a broader perspective of a player's true instinctive abilities within a team structure. I needed this because as a Draftnik I am at a disadvantage not having the information on a player that NFL teams have. I knew that by watching the whole game that a player would most likely show his true character, football intelligence, and overall positive and negative intangibles. The scouts, GM's and coaches use what they call the "Coaches Film". I have seen that film but being at a disadvantage of not working in that professional world, I need film that shows me the whites of player's eyes, so to speak. I need to see and get an impression of what a player is thinking and feeling during the course of a game. I needed to see if an offensive lineman who pulled out late one time was showing more of an effort when he pulled the next time in spite of the fact he might be using the incorrect techniques or was still too slow.

I know the amount of time and money that I'm able to invest on the draft doesn't come close to the amount of time or money an NFL team spends. I also know that we Draftniks cannot profile a player in the same way an NFL team profiles a player. NFL teams start with an enormous amount of off & on field information on a player. Draftniks like me, have to work from film first and then collect what information we can gather on a player to add to a profile.

In truth, it doesn't matter how a person goes about profiling a player but for me, I just want the college seniors name and number to evaluate a player on film first. Collecting information on a player's size and speed along with any other information comes later in the process. I am limited to doing about 120 to 140 profiles a draft season and use Rob's ever changing top 100 lists throughout the pre draft process to stay focused on the players that most fans and other Draftniks are interested in. That does not prevent me from profiling any player I wish to profile nor those who stand out on film. It does however, keep the profiles limited to players that fans and other Draftniks are most interested in knowing about. If I profile a player and they never make

Rob's top 100, so be it. That doesn't change what I saw on film. It just means there might be a player in the draft that is being overlooked.

Right or wrong, this way of profiling allows me to be free of the influence of outside sources on player's talents to play for the NFL. It also gives the fan a clean look at a player without any prejudice or any emotional attachment to a player on my part. I'm just a guy in a room looking at film. I feel no pressure to be right or wrong about a player because all I can do is communicate to you what I see. Being right or wrong about a player is always debatable.

After looking at film, I gather other information to see if it jives with what I see. I am a firm believer that problems a player might have personally can show itself in the player's play on the field, if you look for it. For example, the character of a player in times of adversity is a very good key to how well a player handles adversity in their personal life. When you gather off field information that doesn't fit what you see on film, I have to trust the film over the outside information. The reason is simple, Draftniks have no way to verify the quality of the outside information. I learned a long time ago working for politicians, that even "verified" information could be wrong information.

I do profiles this way out of necessity and also because all of us fans have been told by the true experts that the film doesn't lie. That being said, my theory for Draftniks is, trust what you see in a players play on the field over information that could be embellished or falsified from off the field. Don't get me wrong I believe in gathering off field information; what I am saying is that a player's play on the field can reflect that players off field behavior. You must use both aspects (on field talent and off field information) and examine how the two are alike, or not alike, to gain the best overall perspective on a specific player.

In doing profiles that addressed character issues from film, I knew I had to come up with some standards. These standards would allow me to organize my thoughts and take note of a player's mental toughness, attention to details, mental strength and all the other intangibles that make a person successful in life. The problem is the intangibles that will set a player apart from others are the most difficult to identify and measure. I knew that setting up some standards would be difficult but not impossible. I started out with the premise that profiling football players is no different from hiring in the business world. Your resume would be equal to a players stats and would pique the employers interest for interviewing a person to see how they would fit into your business. But no matter what the resume said the hiring relied on the interview. For me personally and as you may know by now, I have to touch it, feel it and see it to get an understanding of it, and watching film does all of that for me and serves, in this case, as a good enough substitute for an interview.

That being said, to help with the film reviewing I decided that I had to treat this process more like a stockbroker on Wall Street who breaks down a business from information and sources available. This includes using film, information, and stats to cumulate a player's ability to play in the NFL. I knew that because of the lack of being able to interview I could not just watch film. I had to "read" the film, looking for a player's level of heart, execution, avidity (desire) and talent (H.E.A.T.).

After establishing a player's physical ability to play in the NFL, I look at film for the following H.E.A.T, standards. I believe this helps me measure a player's mental toughness and gives some insight into their on and off field football character.

H. E. A. T. Profile Standards

Heart—What the player shows on film in the 4th quarter of a winning and losing game situation. Does the player have the character to win and lose with sportsmanship?

Execution—How well the player executes the game plan and the specific responsibilities of his position. Does the player (based on execution) make impact plays during the course of a game?

Avidity—Does the player on film take downs off? Does the player have stamina in the 4th quarter? Does a player (based on effort) make impact plays during the course of a game and in the 4th quarter?

Talent—Does the player show on film the speed, strength, balance and awareness needed to be a success at the next level? Does his skill improve from year to year? How does his production/stats relate to his talent? Does the player (based on talent) make impact plays during the course of a game?

Looking at film for me includes evaluating the way a player conducts himself with coaches and teammates on the sidelines in good times and in bad. To most people reading this right now, you might be saying to yourself, "Yeah, right! He can see all of those things?" Well all I can say to that is, yes. I can and do see all of those things about a player from the film and so do most of the fans and fellow Draftniks. The average fan and Draftnik may not have written guidelines or even understand the reasons why they don't like a player. But in reality when voicing an opinion of a player they have seen play, they have formed a rudimentary profile based on their own life experiences and learned ability to "read" people.

Everyone's life experiences will differ and I will admit some of my life experiences are a little out of the norm, but the requirement for reading people is not the "type" of life experiences, just the fact you have them.

I think for me working with animals at a very young age gave me a unique insight into reading people earlier than then most. As strange as that sounds, almost anyone who has worked with animals will tell you, that comparison is not strange at all. Both species are born with natural abilities that are different from each other for example, the hunting dog who knows how to naturally hunt and flush a bird as compared to the dog the naturally herds. That's comparable to a person born with the ability to sing or the natural ability to calculate from the person who has natural athletic abilities. All species are born with different naturally abilities and respond to habits and direction to develop those natural abilities. The major distinction between human beings and animals is the ability of the human being to think as an individual and to expand on our natural talents and develop other natural abilities. My experiences with animals may be a different way of acquiring and developing the knowledge needed to "read" people but for those of you who work with animals understand it's not that strange.

My first job at 15 years old was literally, shoveling crap and cleaning up after three elephants Dolly, Daisy, and Daffodil. Working around these large impressive mammals allowed me to develop the knowledge that influence and control is not based in physical intimidation. When it comes to motivating a five-ton elephant to do a trick or to follow you calmly to a water hole 500 yards away from its sleeping quarters, physical domination by a human is impossible to use as a control mechanism. What does work is gaining control of the animal by reading the animal's physical behavior to predict mood and future behavior. A good trainer is able to gain control by studying the animal's mannerisms and body movement. Taking note of the animal's patterns of emotional response to its environment and then taking control of the environment. Yelling and demanding just doesn't do it. How many of you have ever stood, twenty feet from an elephant that has turned in fear and is about to grab someone and fling them ten feet into the air? Not many, I imagine. I can tell you it is a freighting experience and if you see it happen, you will never forget it. The power of that beast makes you feel so insignificant that you never forget that feeling ever again. I am happy to say, as a 15 year old kid and through all of my teen years I was kept out of danger because of an excellent trainer who kept me safe and Dolly, Daisy and Daffodil happy.

One of my many other jobs after graduating High School was in stark contrast to my days with the animal show. I worked for a fast food franchise in the Bronx. For those of you who might not realize, the Bronx has 1.4 million people living in 42 square miles. It has been designated, by the U.S. Census Bureau as the area with the most diverse population in the United States. This job taught me how to understand and deal with kids and the public from the poorest neighborhoods in this country. Believe it or not, in difficult situations I used much of what I learned from being around those elephants. I knew physically trying to dominate people was not going to work. Let me tell you this, having a gun held to your head by a kid coming down off drugs with the shakes will give you that same insignificant feeling.

In the following years, I came to develop and value that skill to read behavior. I continued to apply this skill in every job that I had for the simple reason that it helped me to stay a step ahead of my peers and impressed my supervisors. I believe every promotion that I have ever received was because of my ability to read people quickly, to evaluate their character, strengths and weakness, and to communicate in an educated fashion.

Now, I don't think the skill of reading people is anything special. In fact, I believe that most observant people who understand how to sell a product, negotiate for a business or deal with the public have to learn how to read people. To be a good politician, police officer, salesperson, lawyer, teacher, executive, housewife or, for that matter, any customer relations job that deals with the public requires you to be good at reading people. That being said, most Draftniks have had jobs that require them to read people. Therefore it's only natural that when a Draftnik watches a player on TV, they automatically form an opinion based on the same subconscious guidelines used to profile a customer or client.

The frustration for a Draftnik is seeing a lack of this important talent in some of the scouts, GM's and coaches of our favorite teams. Draftniks and fans see the obvious mannerisms that tell us a player is full of BS. We see it because we deal with it in our everyday lives. Anybody can see a player on TV and tell if that player has better talent than another player. The question is can you see, in their play on the field, if he will be a good NFL player or if that player is full of crap. Profiling is not about projecting, it's about indentifying; indentifying in the present how a person is mostly likely to react when put in the same situation in the future.

Talent evaluation is an art all to itself. It has nothing to do with whether you have played the game of football or have coached it professionally. Ask yourself this question, "Are all doctors' good surgeons?" Relate this question to whether or not great position coaches are great head coaches, or if great quarterbacks are great quarterback coaches. Similarly, talent evaluators are good at evaluating talent but that doesn't necessarily mean they were ever good athletes or good coaches or vice versa. Now there are always exceptions to this, but to assume that everyone who is a coach or GM or scout is good at reading people or is good at their job because they work in the NFL is ludicrous.

Let's take for example Head Coaches. This group of people insists on selecting their own players for the draft. According to his Wikipedia page the expression Bill Parcells used before he quit as head coach of the New England Patriots in 1996 was "They want you to cook the dinner; at least they ought to let you shop for some of the groceries". Here's the problem with that statement, a lot of chefs think they can cut corners and substitute a lower grade of vegetables because their cooking skills can make up the difference. It can happen once but those chefs are fooling themselves if they think they are going to put out a good product meal after meal with that theory. This thinking is similar to a coach who thinks he can "coach a player up" when that player has proven to have less than the needed intangibles to succeed. It can happen for a game or two but not for a season or the length of a full contract.

There is a conflict of interest right off the bat when a head coach is selecting players for the draft. Most coaches are interested in one thing and one thing only, themselves! That's not a criticism, its realty. A good coach is ego driven to be the best. They look at the draft from the prospective of collecting the best talent. They believe they can't teach talent but can "coach up" everything else. My belief is a player's ability to impact does not come just from talent, it comes from his character and intangibles and without them a player will never live up to his talent. Now before we go any further there are exceptions to every rule and there are some very fine Head Coaches who have proven over the years to be good talent evaluators. I'm are not talking about that minority. I'm talking about the majority.

The problem for the majority of coaches in evaluating players for the draft goes beyond this conflict of interest. Coaches are affected by the natural make up of the position of Head Coach and its dictatorial nature. Coaches will tell players and teach players what to do and then expect them to do it. That's not a knock on coaches but it's why most coaches are not good draft evaluators. Coaches struggle to read people because it is not a requirement of their job. The truth is I believe a coach's wife would be better at reading people in most cases then they are. Coaches live for their jobs and most are socially inept except with each other. The normal "reading" people skills have been stunted because of the cocooning nature of the job. If you are an NFL coach it's almost like being a part of a secret society. Everything is done for them and all they have to do is coach. The wives take care of all of the family needs. They pay the bills, do the shopping, take care of the children and are the stabilizing factor of the family. The agent takes care of the contracts and the team feeds them and clothes them. They live to work and reading people is not a requirement for them to "succeed" in their work.

Another problem I suspect coaches have that affects their ability to evaluate players for the draft is in the breaking down of film. Breaking down film for coaching techniques requires a different skill set than "reading" film to evaluate talent. A Coach looks at film to see how they can improve a player by teaching him new techniques. I'm looking for why that player hasn't learned those techniques especially if he has been playing for two or three years. Is it because of bad coaching or the system the player plays in or because the player lacks the needed intangibles for the NFL level? Most coaches are looking at film of a player for ways he can improve a player. I'm trying to read in his play if a player wants to improve himself. That is the difference in breaking down film for coaching and reading film to evaluate talent. It's a mind set.

Many coaches in the NFL think they can select talent for the draft, and many are no longer coaching or have had to take a step back to a coordinator position. This step back in a coaching career happens (in most cases) because of a failed 1st round selection in previous drafts. How do I know this? The History of 1st round draft bust proves it and, therefore, proves my point that many coaches have too many overlapping responsibilities when it comes to the draft. In my mind a coach's responsibility in the draft is to evaluate a group of players who have been pre selected by the scouts and GM based partially on a coaches wish list to improve the team position wise. A coach would interview those players at the combine to identify a player's ability to except coaching, how a player will fit into the system that he runs and for locker room continuity. Scouts and GM's responsibilities are to evaluate talent based on the ability of a player to fit into any type of system, character, intangibles, instincts, football intelligence and rate them according to whatever rating system talent wise they use. Than a GM and Head coach sit down and evaluate those players on the value of the position they play on the team along with team needs and what rounds they think are appropriate to draft that player. Too many head coaches want to get involved in the talent portion of the process and that to me is where they problem exist. Of course this is just in Drew's perfect world of drafting.

Year after year we go through players selected in the 1st round that fail because of character issues and lack of intangibles. To prove my point, below is a list of players from 1999 to 2009 who were selected as the <u>very first pick</u> of their drafts and considered the best players of those drafts respectively.

1999—Tim Couch QB Browns, 2000—Courtney Brown DT Browns, 2001—Michael Vick QB Falcons, 2002—David Carr QB Texans, 2003—Carson Palmer QB Bengals, 2004—Eli Manning QB Chargers, 2005—Alex D Smith QB 49ers, 2006—Mario Williams DE

Texans, 2007—JaMarcus Russell QB Raiders, 2008—Jake Long LT Miami, 2009—Matthew Stafford QB Lions

As you can see, this list includes players who have had no success, have had marginal success, and those who have had great success. You can decide who falls into what category for yourself.

We are told that every one of these players took the Wonderlic Test, went to the combine, were scouted for years and were interviewed by coaches, GM's, and owners. We are told that background checks are done on every one of them from the womb to their present drafts respectively.

Let's all think about this for a minute, if all of this off field information is gathered about the first pick in the draft and there is proof of their talent, then I have to ask one question. Why are there so many players chosen first in the draft that do not live up to expectations in the NFL? The answer is, the teams drafting at the first slot in the draft, obviously put a higher priority on talent. That suggest that head coaches are having too much say in the draft and in prioritizing talent over character, history proves this is a big mistake.

Let's look at some of these players from a character/ talent comparison and you tell me. If you consider Carson Palmer better than Michael Vick, is it because of athletic talent, height or who can throw the ball farther? With the talent both of those players have I would think if you consider one player better than the other it will be because of who has the better intangibles, like game management skills, decision making under pressure, handling adversity and leading others when adversity strikes during a game. Does Eli Manning QB New York Giants have more success than Alex Smith QB San Francisco 49 ER's because he throws the ball better or has a stronger arm? No, it's because of his intangibles, leadership and football intelligence.

41

Did JaMarcus Russell fail because of a lack of talent, bad mechanics, or because of a lack of character and intangibles causing a poor work ethic, football intelligence and decision making abilities? Is the real reason David Carr failed as a possible franchise QB because of his release point? I don't think so. Did Courtney Brown not have enough talent to be successful or did he lack the intangibles to be successful? The truth is, not one of the players on that list failed because of a lack of talent and most likely were drafted with the thinking that the coaches could "coach up" work ethic, character, mental stamina and football intelligence. They thought this because they were enamored by that beautiful spiral thrown 70 yds down the field or the explosion off the line that was quicker than anyone else in workouts or because a quarterback ran a pro offense at the college level. I don't believe it's the responsibility of an NFL coach to draft a player and have to "coach up" his intangibles.

An NFL coach does not have the time to teach the intangibles at the NFL level. That's like hiring a person for your firm out of college and being involved in their personal life outside of work. Who does that? Nobody expects people to be perfect, we all make mistakes. Drafting players on talent, however, while ignoring how a player handles those mistakes tells me you just spent a boat load of money and time for nothing. There is a saying, I think Rob said it to me once, "Draft a meat head and chances are you won't get steak, all you'll get is beef jerky." A player must have the character and intangibles already in place on draft day. Good profilers need to be able to read those qualities on film along with the necessary level of talent required to be successful. On field talent and off field behavior are reflections of one another.

I believe a true profile is a snap shot of how a player is playing the game at that time in his life. You are using triggers in a game to give you a picture of how that player will recast and react to that same situation at the next level. If you "read" the film correctly you will also see how a player reacts to situations of adversity and that will give you insight into a player's character and intangibles. If you believe, as I do, about character and intangibles being as important as talent then you can see why it is difficult for a coach to see past a player's talent. It's just not in his nature.

Doing profiles this way is not perfect, but I think "reading" the film instead of just looking for talent and matching it with outside information, is the best way for me.

The skill to evaluate players for the NFL can come from any type of person with any type of background as long as that person possesses the ability to read people. That's why a Draftnik sitting in a room looking at film can be just as good at analyzing players for the NFL as any media type or NFL personnel. That may piss a lot of people off who work in the NFL but that is the truth. Profiling a player for the NFL is not just about the measurement of athletic talent, it's also about the measurement of player psychology and I believe that Psychology is hidden on film in how a player plays, not in just his ability to play.

There are teams in the NFL that draft well every year. Those are the teams that have developed a consistency in their management skills and draft guidelines. They have good owners, who allow smart GM's, who allow excellent coaches who allow outstanding scouts, to all do their jobs together with no overlapping responsibilities. Those teams also understand people, along with the self motivation skills a player has to have to be successful in the NFL. They don't gamble but they will take calculated risks.

In taking calculated risks they first establish the talent needed to play the position at the NFL level and then move on to evaluating the intangibles that are just as important. Remember, the draft is about selecting players who understand how to use their talents and will continue to develop those talents. It's about selecting players who can take what they learn in practice and have the discipline to apply it in a game with success. It's about football intelligence and that can be different from book smart intelligence. Looking at film and identifying these issues in a player's play on the field is what profiling is all about. It is not about collecting information and then reporting that information as a profile.

The difference between me and most everyone else who profile players for the fans is, I believe the talent in everyone I profile is the easiest part of a player to evaluate. It's a given. A player either exceeds or meets those athletic standards or they don't. I know athletic testing is a way to verify physical stamina and weed out potential underline medical issues but all teams should know how athletic a player is by the time they are invited to the combine. In most cases, scouts have been working out targeted players since their freshman season. Sometimes a player will go to the combine and surprise you with some slow times that you didn't expect. That's when you go back to the film and look to see how fast that player plays. Some guys are just not good at running track, but they can run fast enough when it means something to them.

The continuing over testing of a player's athletic talent is not solving the problem of who can be successful at the NFL level. Understanding how to "read" film and indentify the intangibles that will make a player successful is the only way to cut down the amount of failed draft selections. Think about it, do you really think the Arizona Cardinals drafted Larry Fitzgerald and cared how fast he ran forty yards? They drafted Larry based on his film, how he played the game, and his intangibles. His forty times was slow by wide receiver standards. I know of no team in the NFL that ever asks them to run forty yards to see if that player has lost any of his speed from when they first drafted him. At the NFL level only the players with strong intangibles have the ability to improve beyond their athletic talents and that is what makes them impact players.

Once you have established that athletic talent, move on. Don't re-test what you already know and gum up the works. Remember when looking at film of a player look for what he brings to the table beyond his talent because, as I always say, it takes more than athletic talent to play in the NFL.

Here is my non expert suggestion to the NFL. If you want to train scouts to be more than information gatherers, than make young scouts take courses that teach them to read body language, behavior, faces, eyes and emotions. Take them to a police interrogation unit and teach them how to identify when a person is lying to another person's face. Teach them to anticipate behavior from player's actions on the field. Don't have them learn techniques of the different positions; they can pick that up by themselves. Teach young scouts how to "read" film and not just look at film as a coach would. Teach them what I learned from Daisy, Dolly and Daffodil.

To complete the last part of your Draftnik training I feel obligated to alert the fans and fellow Draftniks to the intimating expressions used by former coaches, players, GM's and media types that have no real meaning but are used all the time for the sole purpose of suggesting that because we Draftniks do not know this special language we can't possibly be smart enough to evaluate players. Some of these expressions I have eluded to in this chapter but now I'll explain to you the hidden meanings behind them.

The first use of an expression that means nothing but is used to intimidate us is the suggestion that a player has "good bloodlines". Now

I know and you know there have been families that have produced very good NFL football players. My problem is, how is that a part of any profile if you are profiling by film? Nobody is automatically as talented or has the same character as their parents or siblings. Even twins have different strengths and weakness and should be evaluated separately.

To suggest in a profile that a player with a former parent or sibling who has played in the NFL has a better chance than most everyone else in that particular draft because of an imaginary bloodline is just nuts. It is tantamount to suggesting if a young college student is the commissioner's son that means he has royal blood and will be the next commissioner. To me there is an obvious subliminal message suggesting to all the other NFL personal that we coached this boy's father or brother so now we must pay those former players back and draft this son or sibling to show solidarity. It sure as hell has nothing to do with talent. When I look at film of a player, I can't see a player's bloodline, even if he has an open cut. I can't read it in body language or mental toughness. The truth is, you could get more out of reading someone's palm, than drafting players based on bloodlines. The expression does not belong in a profile at all because it has no value to the player. In fact in some cases it can be a detriment. What's next, drafting children from the womb of the wives of former NFL players? All I can say is, don't ask me to look at that film.

Another expression that drives me nuts is the suggestion that if a QB plays in a certain style of offensive system that means he will not be (or will be) successful in the NFL. I don't profile systems, I profile players. To me, this is a copout statement and just means the scout or coach is afraid to give a profile that might be wrong. It's a total copout, plain and simple.

Of course it would be thoughtless of me if I didn't circle back and revisit this next expression that just makes me want to scream at the TV when I hear the words; "we feel that we can coach him up". This statement is uttered after drafting a player who has excellent talent but has underachieved at the college level. As far as I'm concerned, that statement really means, talent is more important than being lazy, dumb, and immature. This statement is used to intimidate us Draftniks into not believing that our favorite team has just screwed up big time in drafting that player.

Not to beat a dead horse but I will. If your first pick in the draft needs "coaching up" to be motivated on the field, then chances are he will need "coaching up" to be motivated off the field to make good decisions. If I owned an NFL franchise and my coach suggest that I needed to pay extra money to hire a "mommy" to follow around our first round draft choice because he needs off field "coaching up", that coach is not drafting for my franchise anymore. He may be a hell of a coach but he has proven that he is only interested in collecting talent and not in building a team. The strangest part of all of this is the team that drafts this underachieving player is convinced they just selected the steal of the draft! What can I say?

Most Draftniks have good instincts when it comes to the draft but still maintain a lack of confidence in evaluating. This lack of confidence is brought about mostly by the media, who insist that they are the only experts qualified to evaluate talent for the NFL draft. That's wrong to assume, just like its wrong to assume a Draftnik doesn't know what he is talking about because he doesn't work in the NFL. On the other hand, there are Draftniks who are not very good at what they do either. Everyone needs to be held accountable when they do a job and no one is automatically an expert at that job just because they do it. At least that's what my life experiences have taught me.

Chapter V

The Ingenious
Two Board System

After I joined THR, I learned more about the inner workings of the draft than I realized had ever existed. Up until that time I just evaluated physically & collected mentally, who I thought were the most talented players and then tried to figure out what round they would be drafted in. The nagging question for me was always why there was better talent picked in the later rounds of the draft then in the earlier rounds of the draft. I saw the talent and I didn't think I had any special abilities that allowed me to evaluate talent better than scouts and GM's, so why did this anomaly occur in every draft? Some might suggest the answer lay in my suspicion that team's weigh talent over the intangibles but that didn't answer the whole question.

Rob Esch, the founder of THR, was the one that came up with this idea of a Two Board System. He understood that teams could, and did, value certain positions differently in the draft and those values could dictate the rounds a team might pick a player in, provided the player had the talent. He based slotting players on his value board, using this "value of position" information along with many other variables. One of those variables include the evaluation of talent and that lead to Rob asking me to put talent board ratings (TBR) on the profiles to add as a variable on his board. The truth is, because I could not touch this idea, or see it, or feel it, I had no idea what Rob was talking about and how it might answer the question of why talent selected late in the draft was sometimes better than some of the earlier picks. In spite of not understanding where Rob was going with his two board idea, I started putting TBR grades on the profile. Without realizing it the two board system was exactly how I used Rob's board before I joined the site. I would target the players I liked for my favorite team and then look at Rob's board to establish what round they most likely would be drafted in. In a rudimentary way I was using the two board system before we decide to use it on the site. But it was Rob who brought it to life and understood the impact of it. So, I just went along for the ride and proceeded to put talent board ratings on the profiles despite the fact that I was not sure what he was trying to accomplish.

Since I struggled to understand what Rob wanted from these talent grades, it was inevitable that I would make mistakes. For the first few years, I was putting a talent board rating that coincided with the round and talent I thought a player would most likely be drafted in by 32 teams. That's what every Draftnik tries to do; we try to predict what round a player might be drafted in and then give a profile that fits that round. This, inadvertently, influences our profiles and affects the true talent and profile of a player. What Rob wanted me to do was put a talent board rating that coincides with a player's talent and what round I would *personally* draft that player in, as if I was a GM.

Having the freedom of suggesting to everyone what round I personally would draft a player in was not going to be that easy for me. Something I learned before I joined the site is that slotting a player is truly a conflict of interest for me. It's a conflict of interest for any talent evaluator or scout because we can't make the decision of value over talent. The reason for this is, all we see is talent and to us, talent is the value. Most scouts are only interested in being correct about a player's ability to be successful in the NFL and the truth is the needs of the franchise are secondary. They don't mean to put the franchise second, they can't help themselves. I truly I'm the same way. I just want the profile to be right and I don't care what round a player is drafted in. That's why I can't do mock drafts very well. I can't pass on a player I think will have an immediate impact, just to go along with who "experts" agree is the safer or more popular pick. So, now you can see why I originally gave up trying to predict what round a player might be drafted in. I hope now you can also see how this new found freedom of rating a player in what round I would personally draft him in, might be very hard to adjust to.

The beauty of the Two Board System is that it puts both value and talent on one board and addresses the main concerns of both scouts and head coaches while still keeping them separate from one another. The two board system shows everyone on the draft management team the talent and value of every player in every round.

Think about it in these parameters, for THR I'm the equivalent of a scout and Rob would be the equivalent of a general manager. The difference is that Rob's value board has to reflect the thinking of 32 head coaches and GM's and not his own views. I try to profile a player for all 32 teams, put a TBR grade on the profile and hand that profile to Rob. I do not involve myself in the value board and Rob doesn't tell me if he thinks I'm wrong about a profile. We keep away from overlapping jobs that cause confusion. If we had a coach for the site then he would be responsible for targeting players that fit his coaching system and the team as a whole. That's how a draft team has to work and this two board system shows everyone how that can be accomplished.

All any NFL team has to do before the draft is take Rob's value board and add their own talent board to it and they will find talented players throughout the entire draft. In doing so, teams will begin to see the possibilities to trade up and be able to anticipate better what other teams might do. This gives teams an advantage they never had before and helps to minimize the guessing they have to do on draft day.

After the first year of adding the TBR grades to the profile, I started to understand more of what Rob wanted. Old habits are hard to break and I would, inevitably, revert back to the old staple of guessing where I thought a player would be drafted rather than where I would draft him. As a result, on the 2007 JaMarcus Russell profile I made the mistake of putting a 1st round TBR grade on the profile when I should have put a 4th round TBR grade on it. I covered myself in the profile by telling everyone that I had deep concerns about JaMarcus mental stamina and work ethic but for the purposes of the two board system putting a 1st round TBR grade on his profile defeated the purpose of indentifying a potential 1st round bust. On draft day you don't have time to read a profile of a player before you draft him so having the information at hand is important. When you see a player on the board and he has a 4th round TBR attached to his name you know you can go to the next player if you chose to. Without the correct TBR grade on the value board you're lost.

The two board system (when done correctly) gives you more insight into what is really happening at that time on draft day. In my opinion not using the THR's two board system on draft day is like going into building on fire with a garden hose and expecting not to get burned. Rob's value board helps NFL teams to understand where a player they have an interest in might be drafted. Just like it did for me in the years before I joined THR.

You might be wondering how Rob builds the value board in the first place. It's not secret, it's just difficult. It takes a lot of hard work, time and contacts to develop. It comes from a simple premise of wanting to know were a player is mostly likely to be drafted instead of a personal view of a player's ability to play in the NFL. Rob learned through years of college scouting that every NFL team values positions differently. For example, some teams will value skill positions before line positions. I personally value the Left Tackle position as the second highest position on a team, right behind the quarterback position. Others feel differently. There is no right or wrong method to how a team values positions. Of course this can, and does, change every year with new personnel, offensive and defensive system changes, the amount of players who are draftable at any one position, the positional needs of a team, length of contracts, free agent signings, combine numbers, and free agency losses. Some years even the age of players in the NFL at a position can be a concern in needs and valuing positions. One thing a good value board will not do is reflect or react to rumors. The value board has to be made up of solid information that is gathered and nurtured over the years from contacts in the NFL community as Rob has accomplished. If it didn't, it wouldn't be very valuable.

For the NFL teams that have discovered and use THR's Two Board System on draft day they are enamored with it and every year we try to add a little more information to it with their impute. The value board is not suppose to reflect any one team's way of slotting players. It is supposed to reflect the consensuses of how all 32 teams are slotting their players. The Two Board System is the combination of scientific data working together with the psychological human element of scouting. Success in talent evaluation will still be a three year evaluation but managing the draft on draft day and selecting value can now be measured the day after if a team is using a Two Board System

The following is a list of rules or guidelines that I have established over the years. These rules are ever changing and I add to them all the time. They are how I would look at the information gathered and how

I would attempt to manage a team on draft day. Before I used the two board system many of these guidelines, I would never had thought of because I was drafting just to collect talent. The Two Board System taught me to look at the draft in a different way. It taught me that the draft is not just for collecting talent, its main purpose it to build a team.

Drew's Draft Rules

1. Workouts should confirm what you already know
2. How a player plays the game is just as important as any stat
3. Character is as important as talent
4. Your team will not win if it drafts criminals
5. Numbers don't lie but they don't tell the whole story
6. The combine should be for medicals and interview, not to evaluate talent or second guess the scouts profiles
7. Scouts evaluate talent, they do not draft or slot players
8. Coaches coach talent, history proves most if not all are not good talent evaluators
9. GM's & Coaches place the value of a player to the team: scouts cannot because they are too close to the players
10. Many times scouts are sent out to plant "inside" information to manipulate and gather more information
11. Don't just draft a guard, draft centers who can play guard or guards that can play center
12. Drafting a franchise LT improves three positions on your team. The LT position, LG position and the QB position.
13. Drafting a franchise center improves center, guards and confidence of the rest of the line as well as the offensive coordinator and the QB, and I love drafting offensive lineman.
14. I love drafting offensive lineman but you should be able to find a right guard standing in the checkout line at a Walmart.

15. Pass rushing is not a specialty. It should be included in the evaluation of the DE and LB position in their totality.

16. Tackling, or lack of it, is a priority and first skill to look for when evaluating all defensive positions. A CB can cover like a blanket but if he doesn't want to tackle, he is worthless.

17. Insisting your team has to draft a certain player or the whole draft is a failure is a trap. The two board system shows you the talent in every round.

18. Every round must be looked at like it is as important as the first round. The goal must be to draft value and talent in every round. No more Mr. Irrelevant it's an insult to the player.

19. Bad teams in the top 10 should trade down whenever possible for more picks in the "present" draft and not for future picks. Future picks are for future GM's and coaches.

20. Never trade out of the top ten when you need a franchise QB, unless there are none to draft.

21. Sell the farm (mother, wife included) to move up in the draft if you think a QB is a franchise QB and your team needs one. Just ask for visitation rights for mom and conjugal visits, for the wife.

22. Drafting best player available is nice to say but don't believe it. The facts are most everyone is drafting for needs and draft day trades prove it.

23. If a Head Coach blows the 1st pick in a draft because of character issues you can bet he will be fired in about three years—sometimes sooner.

24. Don't believe in the crap that this is a passing league, There are maybe five franchise QB's in this league, the rest need the threat of a good running game to succeed.

25. WR's and RB's can be found in any round in the draft but there are exceptions to every rule.

26. LB's do not have to run 40 yards in 4.30, they just have to be smart to know how not to get beat by an opponent who can run a 4.30 forty.

Managing the draft on draft day is just as important as collecting the information on the players. You can agree or disagree with anyone of these 26 rules that's not the issue. The issue is if draft is not done correctly then you have wasted a lot of money and time and run the risk of lessoning the overall impact of the draft for your franchise. Remember I'm not out to prove anyone else is wrong, I do this to prove to myself that I'm right.

Chapter VI

Buddy Nix &
Bill Belichick Profiles

"It's not a sin to tell a lie in pre draft talk".

Buddy Nix, General Manager Buffalo Bills, in an interview in March before the April 2011 draft, said it the best and set the tone for the 2011 draft.

To put together a good value board you have to keep track of the General Managers in the NFL. So profiling them seemed only natural to me and might help in setting up a good value board. Besides I would be remiss, if I didn't understand the makeup of a person I have to interact with for business. One of the reasons that made profiling GM's necessary is because the NFL GM's and Head Coaches are famous for giving out misinformation, half truths, and telling white lies leading up to the draft. They believe in it and the opening statement to this chapter by Buddy Nix GM Buffalo Bills before the 2011 draft is proof of it. I call this strategically placed miss-information to the media and fans "The Politics of the Draft". Since this "politics of the draft" existed it seemed reasonable that to be able to cut through the BS, we had to know more about the person delivering it.

Most of us shoot the bull and tell little white lie's. We do it every day of our lives. We do it when we talk with our neighbors, friends, and co-workers with special emphasis on facts that make us look good and little emphasis on the facts that we feel make us look bad. Both men and women tell white lie's, although surveys exposes men as lying more often, with all time favorite lies of, "I only had one drink officer" and "no honey, I don't think your butt looks big in those pants."

Over the years, I have interacted with a diverse group of people who forced me to develop the skill of "reading people" for my own survival.

I have interacted with the uneducated to the overeducated, to folks from the poorest neighborhoods, to the richest neighborhoods, politicians, foreign dignitaries, media, and in between. I've engaged people in just about every walk of life that when you first interact with, have a different goal than just meeting you, an ulterior motive, so to speak. In meeting these people, I have learned to throw the bull when necessary and recognize when the bull or half truths are being thrown. I'm also able to identify the little white lies that people tell. All you have to do is give them enough time to expose themselves and have a good memory. Hence the moniker B S Detector!

After Buddy Nix told everyone not to believe anything he said about the draft prior to the draft, he then proceed to openly feed the media information on Cam Newton QB Auburn who at that time was not being considered as a top ten pick in the 2011 draft. I don't know about anyone else but the red flags were up and flying for me right away. The politics of the draft has become a game within a game for the fans. Most Draftniks don't understand that when they establish a draft website, are successful, and hang around for about five years or more, they will become a part of the politics of the draft. NFL teams and agents will try to influence the Draftniks and media in a way that will benefit them, just like a politician's political campaign. This is all accomplished with the help of a competitive field of news media and so called media experts all fighting to get any story about players or teams first. The code words that drive this sort of bull and white lie's for the draft goes by the name of, "inside information" or "unnamed sources" oh yea and the one that is most effective, "some scouts are saying". When you hear those phrases before a sentence, understand the information you are about to hear is planted for a positive or negative reaction and believe the story at your own risk.

There are two men who are examples in the NFL of people who know how to throw the bull and who are able to tell white lies without blinking. They are Buddy Nix General Manager, Buffalo Bills and Bill Belichick Head Coach, New England Patriots. I watched Buddy Nix in the 2011 draft, work the media and the draft process like a maestro conducting a symphony. The reason I think that Buddy might have had his way in the 2011 draft is because I'm convinced that Cam Newton QB Auburn was not Buddy's top player on his list.

I believe he wanted to draft Marcell Dareus DT Alabama the whole time. My instincts tell me that Buddy's list of his top three players were, Marcell Dareus DT Alabama, Blaine Gabbert QB Missouri, and Cam Newton QB Auburn. I have no way to verify this but two players Buddy did not talk much about unless asked directly were Marcell Dareus and Blaine Gabbert. When Buddy was asked about those two players he talked about them in general and how good they were but kept the passion out of his voice. When he talked about Cam, he made sure the passion in his voice for Cam's talents was obvious.

I may be wrong but I just think Buddy was too obvious and open about Cam. With Buddy it's not about the players he talks about that he is interested in, it's the players he doesn't talk about that he is truly interested in.

Now, I don't know these two men personally, and have never even seen them face to face but for the fun of it, let's go to the film and profile these two personalities.

Buddy Nix General Manager—Buffalo Bills

Buddy Nix reminds me of the carnival workers I worked with in the past. Carnival workers hardly ever lie right to your face and are extremely loyal to family and other carnival friends. On the other hand, a clever and resourceful group, the carnies may have invented throwing the bull and deceiving. According to his bio on the Buffalo Bills site, Buddy Nix started his scouting career in the NFL in 1993 with the Buffalo Bills. At least that's what he admits to. I suspect there is more to this football man than that. His career has brought him full circle back to the Bills with a ton of experience in all aspects of professional football. This experience clearly has taught Buddy how to manipulate the media to his advantage. I love the way he leads the media right where he wants them to go but without giving them any tangible information. Buddy is adept at deflecting questions. If a sport reporter asks a question like, "are the Bills looking at Quarterbacks in the draft", Buddy knows, why that question is being asked, and is prepared for it. I suspect that when Buddy walks into a room full media, he subconsciously profiles everyone who is going to ask him questions. Buddy also uses facial expressions and body language to bluff, emphasize, and add suspicion when he is deflecting questions that pertain to the draft. But a good profiler can read what Buddy is doing if they take the time.

For example, sometimes Buddy will have a scowl on his face and that means he is not giving that person anything of value because they are not to be trusted to report it correctly. Sometimes you will see Buddy become restless and change the way he is sitting in his chair.

59

That means he is measuring carefully what he is about to say and making sure the information he gives is not specific. Sometimes he will smile and tell a joke. When that happens he is feeding, something to someone that he knows is going to be the talk of this press conference and he is smiling because manipulating information to this person is fun. Buddy is a hard worker and don't fall for that old coonhound lying around sunning himself in the Louisiana sun routine, he likes to promote about himself. When Buddy hits that media room, he is working and on the hunt. He is a very smart, instinctive manager who knows how to read and lead people but also knows when to follow. Buddy's "reading people" skills serve him well when profiling players along with dealing with the media. What intrigues me the most about Buddy Nix is his personal commitment to integrity, coupled with the expectation and acceptance that other's may not act with that same integrity. This allows Buddy to accept and deal with people he may not like or respect personally but will deal with them professionally. Buddy accepts the mistakes that he and others around him will make and learns from them very quickly. He is able to turn the page on those mistakes but will not except a lack of effort to correct them in himself or others. He holds himself to the same standards he holds others to and I suspect that Buddy believes in that old saying, "Keep your friends close and your enemies closer". I can relate to that.

If the media happens to paint Buddy into a corner with a question, he will not tell an out and out lie, but he will confuse the issue and at times tell a little white lie. One of Buddy's stock answers to a question he doesn't want to answer might sound something like this, I can't answer that question because if I do you will think that I like that player and If I don't give you an answer, than you will think I don't like that player. Confused? All I can say is Buddy would be a hell of a politician. Buddy runs his office with loyalty, honesty, and privacy. To the people who mirror those traits he is like a father figure. To others who do not show those traits, he will throw the bull and keep them *close but they will not be a part of his inner circle although, he will make them think they are.*

Buddy values QB's, CB's, Pass Rushers (DE), OL, DT's, WR's, RB's, S, but is not married to value when selecting in the draft. Talent & production is the priority and character is always a concern but not a complete deal breaker. Buddy will take a risk on the character of a player if he can convince himself the player will not be a repeat offender. That's his Achilles heel.

Now let's profile Bill Belichick. Both men do an excellent job of manipulate the NFL draft process using totally different methods.

Bill Belichick Head Coach—New England Patriots

Bill Belichick is a horse of a different color. Don't get me wrong, Bill runs his office with honesty, loyalty, and is protective of the people who work with him just like Buddy Nix. The difference is how these two professionals interact with those that do not show those traits back to them.

Bill Belichick deals with the media different than Buddy Nix. He can't be bothered with throwing the bull in public forum. He would rather tell a white lie in private and deal with the consequences later. He prefers one on one situation's because, if he tells a white lie he can keep the backlash to a minimum by saying he was misquoted or taken out of context. In a press conference, a white lie becomes a big problem. Giving a private one on one interview also allows Bill to befriend a media person and control the amount of information he disseminates. This control allows him to deal with the media on his terms while strategically spinning negative and positive tales about players in the draft. I call head coaches like Bill Belichick risk management coaches because that's how they run their teams. Like an insurance company, evaluating the risk of each decision in advance. I imagine that Bill's favorite saying is, "What's the worst that can happen"!

Bill evaluates the risk in both free agency and the draft but is smart enough not to overpay for those risks. He goes to the draft and deals with free agency with the same mentality of a woman snipping coupons to see if she can beat the supermarket out of a $100 dollars worth of groceries for $10 dollars. Bill also treats free agency and the draft together as one entity.

Should the media dare challenge him, Belichick can simply suggest the information is incorrect and that reporter will never have access to the Patriots ever again. Do I know this for a fact? No, but this is a profile and my instincts and the film of Bill at press conferences and how uncomfortable he is suggest this behavior. The fact that Bill also talks in very low tones shows he is very guarded in what he says and does not want to be quoted. In spite of Bill's propensity to tell white lie's I suspect that he keeps his owner in the loop every time he knows he is going to or is in the process of, pushing the rules. I suspect the reason Bill Belichick has been successful running the Patriots over any other team, is because of his honest and open relationship with this owner.

If Buddy Nix runs his office in a patriarchal way, Bill Belichick runs his office as if he is the oldest sibling in the family. The difference is that Buddy will take all the heat when it comes down but Bill needs a parent figure like Patriots owner Robert Kraft to lean on and stand by him when he is caught telling a little white lie or when pushing the rules.

Robert Kraft is a smart man, knows the risk, and has Bills back as long as Bill keeps him in the loop. Bill Belichick does not believe in the saying, "you keep your friends close, and your enemies closer". Once you are accepted to his inner circle you are golden, but cross him, and you're out forever. That goes for players on and off the field also.

Bill Belichick is the type of guy I would want next to me in a foxhole. He is smart, instinctive, and consistent. It seems to me that he is always looking for a new way to do an old thing. He does a good job working the media for a draft and is an excellent coach. I believe at some point draft history will reflect, that along with a few others in the NFL, Bill is behind an enormous amount of positive and negative information leaked to the media in an effect to manipulate other teams perception of players in the draft. Bill's priority in a draft is football intelligence. He will draft a more intelligent player over a more talented player. His value of positions will vary from year to year depending on his needs. He will draft the most football intelligent player available more than he will draft for needs. He prefers to fill his needs in free agency because he feels it's easier to evaluate a professional player than a college player and the risk is less. Most teams work the opposite way. Bill values DL, OL, CB, LB and then the other skill positions. Bill Belichick will trade up if he sees a player with intelligence and talent. The problem is most of the time he finds that combination lacking in most drafts, and will move back and collect picks in future drafts in the hope that at some point that combination will come to fruition. Bill has one weakness, he will draft players who show good intelligence but have made bad decisions off the field. That comes from the fact that he is a coach first and a talent evaluator second. The coach in him always feels he can coach the kid up. That's his Achilles heel.

Both of these profiles are just starting points that I would use when having to meet and deal with these two gentlemen. Future interaction, impressions and dealings would be noted and added to both profiles in future years if needed. How does this relate to the draft? It gives you little insight into the type of players both teams might be interested in drafting and the value of positions and that helps set the value board.

At the start of draft season most of the media will gather the same, starting point information, given to the teams to start their draft process. After that, what drives the changes in player ratings in the media everyday like a stock market, is the "inside information" the media gathers from agents, college players, college coaches, relatives of players and the "white lies" the NFL personal leak. That information is taken from these sources and funneled out to the fans as quickly as a child can slide down a water slide in an amusement park.

Now some of you are reading this and thinking that this "politics of the draft" and planting of negative and positive stories is quite the conspiracy theory! It's a theory based on what I would do if I was a General Manager. As a General Manager I would want to know as much information about what might happen on draft day as possible and I would do just about anything within the rules to gain that information. I would even plant a story suggesting that Cam Newton was not very well liked, just to see how many teams defend Cam and to ascertain what teams are interested in drafting a QB. If setting up an unsuspecting reporter to look like a fool was also accomplished in planting that story that would just be the whip cream on top of the hot fudge Sunday. Fooling everyone into thinking that I wanted to draft a quarterback when I really wanted to draft a defensive tackle would be the cherry on top.

Chapter VII

The Tim Tebow Profile

A Perfect Example of a H. E. A. T. Profile

Those of you, who are members of The Huddle Report.com NFL draft site, know that at some point the challenging, arrogant, obnoxious Drew would show up sooner or later in this book. So strap your seat belt on and get ready for it because here it comes.

As you must know by now, I have this belief that just because you played in the NFL, that does not make you an expert in evaluating players for the NFL. I'm not saying that former players can't evaluate other players. I'm saying being a former player doesn't automatically make you an expert in evaluating players as some media outlets and former players like to suggest. I'm not intimidated by former players who think they know more than the average Draftnik when forming an opinion on the success of a college player. In fact, for me personally I challenge all of them to do what I do. Put your opinions of a players potential in writing and prove it year after year, just like I do. I don't mean this as a statement of arrogance. It is a statement of pride. To help prove my point on this issue I'm willing to put myself out there once again for criticism by all the media experts on Tim Tebow. Most of the former players and media experts who have an opinion about

Tim Tebow have been passionate in there negative critique of him. Most of them see a player that has very bad mechanics and a long release when he throws a pass. Those experts saw that he played in a spread offense and not under center and that was also a real sticking point. These experts also saw a left hand QB and they know that most NFL coaches hate left hand QB's. The biggest sticking point for most media experts in evaluating Tim was that Tim was a QB who runs more than he passes. That surprises me because, these very same experts are enamored with Vince Young and Michael Vick who both are considered running quarterbacks. In general, the experts felt that Tim was not ready to play from the pocket in a typical NFL offense and most felt he will never be a successful NFL quarterback.

My Tim Tebow profile is a perfect example of the difference in breaking down film for techniques as a coach or a former player would do and breaking down film as I do for talent, character and to identify the intangibles a player has to have that make a player successful in the NFL. When I profiled Tim Tebow, I profiled how good I though Tim Tebow would be for the NFL. I profile him using my H.E.A.T. method. I did not profile his coach or his college team or an offensive system I profiled the player. Using my H.E.A.T. standards, I saw the steely leadership skills of the CEO of a fortune 500 company. I saw a person who needs to learn and wants to learn, and has excellent overall athletic talent to play the QB position at the next level. Maybe those athletic skills needed refining but they existed. In Tim, I saw a player who understands the chess game that an offensive coordinator has to play in the way he calls plays during the game. I also saw a player who understood his responsibility to both his team's offense and defense and I saw a quarterback who only took calculated risks at the appropriate times of a game. In spite of the hatred and jealously the media seems to have for Tim I saw a player who is literally loved by his teammates and coaches and the fans in every film I watched and finally coming from an owner's point of view I also saw a marketing aspect to Tim Tebow that was remarkable. I did not need to know Tim personally or find out about his life in general. I did not need to interview his mother or any other family members. All I did was watch how Tim played the game of football and made sure his athletic talent was good enough for the next level.

The draft is very risky but what I saw in Tim Tebow was a good calculated risk and I had no fear in stating my case that Tim would be a very successful NFL as a quarterback or at any other position. In fact I stated that Tim is a franchise player who will develop into a franchise QB. As far as bad mechanic's are concerned, isn't that what coaches are for!

Now some of you will suggest after reading this and the original profile of Tim that I am out on a limb with this profile. Some will say that I will have no credibility if Tim isn't successful in the NFL as a QB. Some will say I have a man crush on Tim and cannot see the truth about him. Those are all statements meant to intimidate me and get me to shut up. I have gone through this many times with my profiles but the reaction this time is very unusual. All I can tell you is this; I consider it an honor to be out on the same limb as Tim Tebow even if he never plays football ever again. As far as my credibility is concerned, I am held accountable for my profiles by the members of the Huddle Report.com and fans of the NFL every year. I don't have any concern at all about the profile I did on Tim Tebow and the fact I rated him as the best player in that draft.

To those former players, who are considered by the media as "experts", they don't do 120 profiles from film every year like I do. It is amazing how they are never held accountable for their expert opinions! I just bet, when Tim becomes successful in the NFL all those experts and former players will suggest they always knew that Tim would make it. Those are the same experts who ridiculed me about my profile on Aaron Rodgers QB Green Bay Packers and insisted he would never make it in the NFL, but now say differently. Like I have said in the past, if you want a reality show about the draft I'll be happy to go up against them all and that is a statement of pride, arrogance or whatever else you might want to call it.

For those scouts, GM's and coaches who make their living off evaluating players as I do, I understand how the fear of being wrong is the biggest reason for second guessing yourselves on Tim. Most real experts profile Tim thinking, that if he is drafted too early and fails, they will lose their jobs. That's a heavy load to carry when you're trying to give an honest profile about a player. I have that load to carry on a much smaller scale, but I do carry the weight of being wrong too much and it affecting the draft site and my credibility. The opinions of those true experts I respect and understand that it is a bit easier for me to go out on a limb than it is for them.

What is really puzzling to me is the adversarial reaction of former players and the media to Tim Tebow. I have to say the negative reaction to Tim personally and his play on the field is nothing short of shocking. You would think that a young man with the character and beliefs in his personal life and his need to succeed in his play on the field would be held up as the role model for the NFL. The strange thing is that Tim is held up as a role model by the fans but the media along with some former players seem to have a jealousy about Tim that goes way beyond the norm. To prove my point, the following is a quote from an article by Mike McCarthy of USA today, dated December 11 2011 about Tim Tebow. It quotes Boomer Esiason former NFL QB about Tim and his ability to play in the NFL.

"He can't play. He can't throw," Esiason said at a CBS press event in New York on Tuesday. "I'm not here to insult him. The reality is he

was a great college football player, maybe the greatest college football player of his time. But he's not an NFL quarterback right now.

"Just because he's God-fearing, and a great person off the field, and was a winner with the team that had the best athletes in college football, doesn't mean his game is going to translate to the NF".

"Tebow's throwing mechanics are so poor, Esiason says, he wouldn't be surprised if the Broncos cut him loose. "What (former Broncos coach) Josh McDaniel saw in him God only knows. Maybe God does know—because the rest of us don't," Esiason said.

I'm not sure if Boomer has a record of profiling players but I am sure of this, Boomer seems to be very upset with the fact that Tim has strong religious beliefs. Boomer also seems to be upset about what he believes to be an influence by the fans in suggesting that Tim might be an excellent NFL player. It seems he takes this influence as a challenge to his talent evaluating abilities. Maybe Boomer is right about Tim and maybe I'm wrong but you would think that former players would know there is always a chance for a player to play in the NFL if they have the talent and intangibles.

I really have no problem with anybody voicing an opinion about any player in the draft. Like I said most of us have some abilities to do just that. I guess my problem is the condescending attitude of these former players when voicing that opinion to the fans. Their attitude is that we have no right to disagree with them on a player's ability because after all, they played the game and that makes them an expert. Well I'm here to say you're not! In fact I'm here to say the average Draftnik watches more film about a college player with an unbiased attitude that you can't possibly have because of your ego and the fact you did play professional football. Later on there was a follow up to this article suggesting that Boomer was now a believer after one of

Tim Tebow's remarkable 4th quarter comebacks, but it was hollow and full of contempt and astonishment that the team Tebow beat allowed him to come back and not because Tim just did a great job. At least that was my impression when I heard him on the air.

Another former player Merrell Hodge, a former fullback for the Pittsburgh Steelers and a self-proclaimed expert in evaluating players for the draft, has decided in Tim's second year in the NFL that he is a bust. It seems for some reason, that Merrell (like Boomer Esiason), has taken a personal dislike to the fans who like Tim. This vendetta against Tim and his fans is strikingly immature and unprofessional but that doesn't matter to hard head Merrell. You would think that Merrell, a former player would see more in the film of Tim Tebow than just a player with bad mechanics. Merrell himself was a player that made it in the NFL with limited athletic abilities. He also fought through a cancer scare. I would think if anyone could see the importance of a player's intangibles it would be Merrell Hodge. Still Merrell's anger is unmistakable! My guess is that all of this anger directed at Tim and his fans is over the fact that Tim was drafted in the first round and that just bugs the hell out of some self proclaimed media experts. I suspect this because one day I heard former wide receiver Chris Carter on the TV suggest, "If Tim had been drafted in the third round instead of the first like he was "supposed to be", none of this animosity would be happening"! So now these so called experts admit that Tim could make it as a third round QB but not as a first round QB! I don't get that thinking at all. What round a player is selected in has no bearing on the success of a player. We prove that with the two board system every year. Like I said before you can't be prejudice and be a good profiler.

Now that I mentioned Chris Carter let's talk about his reaction to Tim Tebow. Chris Carter is a former NFL Wide Receiver who early in his career admitted to alcohol and drug abuse with large amounts of ecstasy and marijuana being his drugs of choice, made an interesting comment the other day when talking about Tim. He said that Tim's "life style" was a hot button. It seems that it's getting harder and harder to play professional football without a drug or alcohol problem or a belief in God, before you commit a crime! After all, as far as these former players are concerned, if you haven't found God in jail, can you truly say you have found God? Seriously, they must believe the only place God hangs out is in the prisons!

Now most of you, like the experts are going to suggest that because I defend Tim that means I have a man crush on him. That's an insult to me. I have never met Tim Tebow and as far as I'm concerned his play on the field speaks for itself. It you don't think Tim Tebow is going to be a good football player at the professional level then that's fine. Attacking me personally is not going to change my mind or intimidate me to shut up. As far as I'm concerned it's the media and former players who need to defend their opinions of Tim as not being prejudiced. They are the ones who do not like Tim because of his religion, life style, and fan base, not me! I like him because of his play on the field and what I see on film. You tell me who's profiles include prejudices and who's do not!

In the same article way down at the very bottom were nobody bothers to read, I think Randy Cross, former NFL offensive lineman said it best. That is unless the media thinks he has a man crush also!

> *"CBS game analyst Randy Cross thinks critics, particularly a hostile news media, are hating on Tebow for wearing his religious beliefs on his sleeve".*

Nevertheless, like a veteran football player hazing a rookie, Merrell Hodge feels the need to show his dominance over the Draftniks and fans who suggest they might know more than him. I can tell you this, there was never any reaction by the media or former player's years ago to Reggie White and his religious beliefs and how he wore them on his sleeve!

I will say this to Merrell, I'll be glad to put my record of profiles up against his any time and once again I do not say that out of arrogance, I say it out of pride. Well maybe a little arrogance! To the rest of the so called media experts, (except for Mel Kiper who always gives a profile on a player based on football), all I can say is your discrimination of players because of their moral beliefs is noted by the fans and me and the fact that when you report anything about Tim in your belligerent and condescending tones it just proves your bias.

For me personally, I think this is a back lash from all of those "experts" who wanted to say truthfully their real thoughts about Vince Young and Michael Vick but felt they could not for fear they would be labeled racist. I have no fear of that because I do on average over 120 profiles from film every year and the film I watch doesn't show racism or discriminates, it only shows talent and character and the intangibles needed to play in the NFL.

I think the best example of a player who came into the NFL and was criticized for his moral beliefs by all the "experts" along with doubts about his talent and ability to play in the NFL was Steve Young former QB San Francisco 49 er's.

According to Steve's Wikipedia page, like Tim Tebow, Steve was a multi talented player who could play more than one position. He was such a great runner that he was heavily recruited by North Carolina, who wanted him to play quarterback in the option offense. Steve decided to attend Brigham Young University because of its passing style offense and his personal religious beliefs. Initially, he struggled at throwing the ball, and BYU's coaching staff considered switching him to defensive back because of his athleticism. Steve wanted to be a quarterback. He worked hard to improve his passing skills and eventually succeeded. In his senior season, Steve passed for 3,902 yards and 33 touchdowns in the regular season, and his 71.3% completion percentage set an <u>NCAA</u> single-season record. He also added 544 yards rushing. With Steve Young at quarterback, BYU set an NCAA record by averaging 584.2 yards of total offense per game. The Cougars finished the year with an impressive 11-1 record.

Steve was named First Team <u>All-American</u> by several news organizations and received the <u>Davey O'Brien National Quarterback Award</u>. He also finished second in voting for the <u>Heisman Trophy</u>. Young finished his college career with 592 pass completions for 7,733 yards and 56 touchdowns, along with 1,048 rushing yards and 18 touchdowns on the ground. He was enshrined in the <u>College Football Hall of Fame</u> in 2001. As a comparison, Tim Tebow finished his college career with 661 completions for 9,286 yds along with a 67.1 % completion rate and 88 passing touchdowns. He also had 692 rushing attempts for 2,947 yds and 56 touchdowns.

I have never been big on stats, but those two player's statistics SCREAM mental toughness and Steve and Tim both proved they had that in deep quantities over the course of their college careers. Steve's professional career started out with the same negatives attached to his play, bad mechanics and all, as Tim Tebow has had to endure. In fact Steve himself has mentioned that his first pass in professional football for the L.A. Express of the USFL in 1984 fluttered so much, he thought it would be shot down by a hunter.

He has been quoted as critiquing his own highlight reel from his early NFL days in Tampa Bay and compares it to the Keystone Cops, with the quarterback running for his football life.

Steve Young was drafted in the 1984 Supplementary draft in the 1st round by the Tampa Bay Buccaneers but did not sign with the Buccaneers until 1985. The Buccaneers posted 2-14 records in each of Young's first two seasons with them, and Steve Young's record as starter was 3-16, in 19 games. Steve threw for only 11 touchdowns with 21 interceptions while completing fewer than 55% of his passes.

In the 1987 draft, The Buccaneers selected <u>University of Miami</u> quarterback <u>Vinnie Testaverde</u> as the first overall pick and Steve Young was officially deemed a bust by all the "experts". Steve was then traded to the San Francisco 49er's on April 24, 1987, to serve as a backup to <u>Joe Montana</u>. In 1993 the 49er's traded an aging Joe Montana to the Kansas City Chiefs after a hall of fame career and Steve Young became the full time starting quarterback. He would go on to become one of the best quarterbacks in NFL history, and earn membership in the Pro Football Hall Of Fame in 2005. <u>Steve Young was the first left-handed Quarterback to be entered into the NFL Football Hall of Fame</u>.

Great players don't necessarily need or have great mechanics. What they do have is the ability to play great and that's what a profiler has to be able to identify when looking at the film. I suspect that Tim Tebow's career just might take a similar path as Steve Young's career did. All I can say to Tim is keep the faith. Fighting adversity is one of your god given strengths.

The following is my original profile of Tim Tebow QB Florida when he came out in the 2010 draft. I listed Tim as a top 10 talent in that draft and thought for sure that the Buffalo Bills at pick number nine or the Jacksonville Jaguars at pick number ten would select him. I was wrong about that but, Tim did get selected in the first round by the Denver Broncos at pick number twenty five and lead the Broncos to the playoffs as the starting quarterback for the first time since the 2005 season.

Tim Tebow QB Florida

STRENGTHS

Tim is a strong powerful multi-talented football player. He has a good strong arm with good accuracy and velocity. He is very smart and understands situational football. Tim is the type of player who leads by example and could motivate a tree to cut itself down to save the rest of the forest. He has improved in all aspects of his game this year. He makes more plays from the pocket than in the past and since his concussion has learned to stay with the play and continue to look down field when flushed from the pocket. He shows excellent touch and accuracy when throwing the deep ball and has improved his feel and touch when throwing to the backs out of the backfield this year. Tim Tebow is mentally strong and athletically talented. He is decisive on and off the field. He loves playing football and loves being in a leadership position and yet he is humble enough and confident enough in his abilities to have the respect of his teammates and coaches.

NEEDS TO IMPROVE

Tim works from a spread offense, does not read defenses, gets all his plays from his coach after his opponent is set, does not look off his hot read, pulls the ball down and runs when his first receiver is covered. When Tim runs he does not set up his blocks, looks for contact, runs too up right, puts his head down and looks for contact . . . and none of these negatives are reasons for me to think that Tim will not be a great QB at the next level . . . because he will!

BOTTOM LINE

Tim is motivated by something that all the great players in any sport are motivated by. Some players need to be the best and to win because that is the only way those athletes can celebrate and repay the talent that has been given to him. Some do it out of respect to their parents who have worked so hard to allow them the chance to be successful. Tim seems to be motivated by both along with the need not to let down his teammates or coaches. There are no negatives to Tim's game that he will not overcome to be the best QB that he can be. He is smart and very coachable and that along with his athletic talent (and his will to be the best player that he can be) is enough for me to tell you that Tim is a franchise QB just waiting to be drafted by a team in need of his talents and leadership. Forget about Tim playing another position. Tim is a natural QB in waiting. Those of you out there who have decided that Tim's negatives outweigh his positives do not understand what it takes to play in the NFL. It takes more than talent to play in the NFL and Tim has so much more than just talent. I call him Tim (Spartacus) Tebow because he will lead your team out of drafting in the top ten.

Chapter VIII

After The Draft Syndrome (ATDS)

Writing profiles and having different reactions from others about a player's potential for the draft is nerve wracking. Trust me, having the ability to read players, understand their potential and having a confident attitude about that ability, seems to antagonize people and makes you a bit of a loner. When I started profiling, I knew I would be criticized for a lack of experience in professional football. That did not deter me. I knew that I had the most important criteria for profiling players for the draft, that being a fan. You can't sit in front of the TV for 30 yrs as a former athlete and not absorb and understand the game of football.

For me the draft is all consuming because of my obsessive work ethic. I put so much time into profiling players that once the draft is over I feel like a junkie coming down off a high, going through withdrawal. This reaction to when the draft has concluded has given me a fictitious disorder that I call "After The Draft Syndrome" or ATDS. Although ATDS strikes most Draftniks after the draft, once struck with this terrible disease, reoccurring episodes can rear its ugly head at any time. The most debilitating aspect of this disorder is the paralyzing sense of doubt, and the urgent need to continue debating the draft. ATDS hits me every year after the draft, like a Tractor Trailer traveling at 65 miles per hour, smashing into a bridge with a clearance of 6.5 feet when the trailer needs 8ft of clearance!

Once ATDS hits, it forces me to interact and even verbally attack strangers on the street. As they desperately try to escape, I frantically explain why I think a player their favorite team just drafted will be successful (or not) in the NFL. It forces me to drive around the backs of restaurants, malls, and office buildings in the hope that some smoker will be outside sucking on a cigarette and be willing to talk about the draft so I can gain some relief from this frustrating solitude.

To my astonishment, I can't seem to find any of the reported 40 million people who watched the draft at all after it is over! Go figure! It almost seems like the 40 million people interested in the draft are hiding from me . . . or could it be my obsessive, overbearing, obnoxious know it all attitude that is putting people off? No, that can't be it!!!

I went to the doctor the other day to talk about this new disorder and I was surprised that the doctors do not have much information on my condition. In light of this, I had no choice but to start wearing a ribbon to draw public attention to this issue, in support of all the Draftniks that are going through this debilitating syndrome. I also went looking for federal funding under the new Obama Health Care Reform Bill but alas, not one politician would take a position and stand up to be counted in the fight for a cure for this terrible disorder. I was very surprised at this lack of action by our political representatives because I know ATDS must be running rapid through the reported 40 million people who watched and were interested in the draft and now, have nowhere to turn to overcome this syndrome. You would think that a disorder that affects over 40 million people in this great country would be a part of the new health care reform bill! I'm just saying! In spite of this confusing attitude about ADTS, I have discovered away to control this disorder but alas, in doing so have brought about a side effect.

Controlling ATDS requires the process of slowly looking at next year's draft eligible players. The truth is looking at that film is like having a woman tell you there is a recall on her birth control pills! Who knows what will happen next? You can look at film but the questions still are many. For example, will the player you're looking at now be injured and out for his senior year? Will the player transfer to another college, be suspended, be arrested, or change his number so I can't find him in his senior year on the film? I suspect like those recalled birth control pills, worrying about what may happen is not going to change a thing and looking at a player's junior season to evaluate his senior season is not going to give me much of a profile either and yet I do it to combat the full force of ADTS.

One of the worst reoccurring ATDS episodes that I have to put up with and try to control involves Tim Tebow.

As you might have already read, I believe that I am the only one in the entire universe who said that Tim Tebow was the best player in the 2010 draft. I also stood steadfast in my prognostication of Tim being selected in the first round of the 2010 draft. Having gone out on that limb, I am prone to ATDS episodes that make me react to any information on Tim's progress like a bull elephant looking for a she elephant in mating season. The information that Tim's rookie jersey was the most selling rookie jersey to date in the NFL proves what I said in my original profile of him. Tim Tebow is a marketing dream.

In the throes of ATDS running rapid through me, every year, I look back to see if I can improve past profiles in any way. I try to improve my writing with more interesting and entertaining comments. I try to make sure that I am communicating clearly, what I see in a player on film. The problem is that once I start looking at past profiles that annoying second guessing aspect of ATDS strikes. Slowly at first, like a cobra standing straight up showing me its hood, swaying back and forth to hypnotize me and then like lightning, the disorder strikes and forces doubt into my psyche. But I fight back with knowledge of film. I realized a long time ago that a profile is a snapshot of a person at a certain time in that person's life. A solid profile factors into the player's personality and character in that snap shot of time, but there will be factors and life events in the player's future that will profoundly affect that player in negative and positive ways. Major life events, like the death of a loved one, or excessive money and fame affect a player's psyche and the player will have to make a decision about how to react at that time when these life experiences happen. A profile of a player is meant as a window into a player's ability to handle those future factors and life events. The fact is until that player handles those life events there is no way to know for sure how he will react. All I can do is suggest how I think he will react based on his play on the field. Not being able to know for certain how a person or player, will react to those conditions is the reason that, no matter how good you might think you are at profiling, there will be plenty of proof to show you are not.

Once ATDS strikes with its demons of doubt, campaigning through the fear of being wrong it can be exhausting and debilitating! I refuse to give into ATDS when it comes to second guessing myself on a profile. I can't change what I see on film just to try to be right all the time but let me tell you, it's a struggle.

Chapter IX

The Dreaded Mock Draft

I am a profiler who studies human behavior for clues about people for a living, and I believe in my own profiles. Mock drafts have always been my biggest weakness and for that reason, I have never liked doing them. All the symptoms of ATDS show up in me when I do a mock draft. I second guess myself all the time and question my own profiles in deciding if players fit certain teams. I go into such mental contortions when I do a mock draft, scientists have asked me if they can open my head to observe my strange behavior during the process. Not being a fan of mock drafts, was not a problem when I was not involved with a draft site but in joining THR, this problem came to an ugly head for me.

Mock Drafts are a significant part of the fun of being involved in the draft. But for reasons I didn't understand early on, I was not having fun doing them for the public. In analyzing myself, I realized that I struggle with doing mock drafts because I have a hard time accepting some of the thinking that some NFL teams use to select draft picks. Once again, this is not a statement of arrogance, it is a statement of reality. If you are doing profiles from film the way that I do than you have to believe in yourself and your work. Now maybe you can see my dilemma when it comes to doing mock drafts. How can I agree with a player being rated as a possible first round draft pick, when I profile from film and rate that player otherwise? It's hard for me to get my head around the fact that some NFL teams just do not see what I see on film about players and I have a hard time doing mock drafts because of it. Now I know that sounds arrogant, but what can I say, it's true. I to fall victim like every other Draftnik, of thinking that I know everything when it comes to the NFL draft. The truth is in calmer circumstances I don't really think I do, but I do have to act like I do. A bit schizophrenic don't you think?

To give you some idea of the emotional struggle I had in completing just one mock draft, the following is a list of players, drafted in the first round of the 2009 draft. I felt these eight players should not be drafted in the first round based on what I saw on film and profiled.

The 2nd selection of Jason Smith OT Baylor drafted by the St Louis Rams

The 3rd selection, Tyson Jackson DT LSU drafted by the Kansas City Chiefs.

The 6th selection, Andre Smith OT Alabama selected by the Cincinnati Bengals.

The 8th selection Eugene Monroe OT Virginia by the Jacksonville Jaguars

The 11th selection, Aaron Mayben DE/LB Penn St by the Buffalo Bills,

The 14th selection, Malcolm Jenkins DB, Ohio St by the New Orleans Saints

The 16th selection, Larry English DE/LB, Northern Illinois, San Diego Charges

The 17th selection, Josh Freeman QB Kansas St by the Tampa Bay Buccaneers

This list is not about who's right or who's wrong. Some of these players have done very well and some have not. The list of eight players who I felt should not be thought of as first round players, is meant to show you that if I stay true to my profiles I would not have listed any of these players in my mock draft. Now maybe you can see my dilemma! On draft day no one really cares if I think a player should be listed, or drafted in the first round. If I complete a mock draft that goes out to the public without the names of the players most likely to be selected in the first round in the upcoming draft do you know what I will receive from my fellow Draftniks, a big fat who gives a crap!

After I joined THR I knew I would have to find away to improve my mock drafts. In profiling my own egregious attitude about mock drafts, I discovered Mock Drafts are not about who I think should be selected in the first round. They are about who is most likely to be selected by the NFL teams in the first round. I assure you that statement is very difficult for me or any true Draftnik to say and accept.

No matter what level of Draftnik you are, everyone likes to participate in a mock draft. Because there are different levels of draftniks, I realize now that a part of my responsibility is to identify for everyone the names of the players who most likely will be selected in the first round and not worry about what I think of those players' abilities for the next level. I finally understood that mock drafts are not about me. They are not about my credibility as a profiler. After indentifying my problem, I decided to combat the issue by doing a mock draft every week of the last month leading up to the draft, along with a final mock that I entered in the THR mock draft contest. This new strategy worked to change my attitude but not to change my accuracy in scoring and making better mock drafts. To this day I suck at doing mock drafts. I blame it all on ADTS and the conflict and struggle I have separating film work from it. Nevertheless, I am proud to say once again ATDS has been beaten back as far as my attitude in doing mock drafts. That is for the time being. To keep this dreaded dysfunction from stopping me from doing any Mock Drafts in the future I will continue to do numerous ones every year, good or bad. I would suggest that you ignore them all or you too may catch ATDS.

Chapter X

It's only Fair,
Drew Boylhart Profile

I think since I profile everyone else that it's only fair for me to profile and analyze myself for you. Some people might suggest that profiling yourself is a bit of a conflict of interest but the truth is, to find out who you really are you must do this. Draft day is a very emotional day and you must understand yourself to effectively negotiate your way through the emotions of the day.

Drew Boylhart Senior Analyst—The Huddle Report.com

Drew is a different person in public than he is in private. In private he has a sniper mentality. He is a bit of a loner along with being organized with some technical expertise and is a meticulous planner. In public he is engaging, a bit of a jokester, witty and if he chooses to be the focal point and in control, can be the life of the party. This chameleon like personality is a perfect fit for a profiler. It allows him in public to disarm a person he meets with jovial conversation as he evaluates unsuspectingly the type of person they are.

Drew strikes me as an honest person who will do business with a hand shake because of the confidence he has in himself to quickly analyze a person. At the same time he understands the need for contracts to confirm that hand shake. He is a person who is smart enough to know that his way is not the only way. I would suspect his favorite saying would be, "If you see a fork in the road take it" because different people will have different interpretations and he likes to promote a state of confusion around him so he can feel in control.

He struggles to accept people who are not honest and is impatient with anyone who has a passion to make things more difficult than they are for the sole purpose of making themselves feel more important. He doesn't accept lying because he feels there is always another way NOT to tell the truth.

Although Drew admits to difficulty in learning and a lack of a quality education he has learned how to appear very smart. This ability to appear very smart seems to be the drive that makes him focus on a task with maniacal like passion.

He is adept at communicating issues and breaking them down into the simplest terms for everyone to understand. To his friends he is loyal, honest and will protect them but at the same time is difficult to get along with. To his enemies he is a street fighter willing to do just about anything within the legal limit of societal thinking. Like Bill Belichick he is a very sore loser but also like Bill, when he loses he blames no one but himself, agonizing over the things he thinks he should have done better. Drew never truly believes that anyone has beaten him. He always believes he didn't do enough to win. Like Buddy Nix he accepts everyone for who they are and never expects more from them then he expects from himself. I do see this about Drew, he is maniacal about communicating correctly what he sees on film about a player. He also will not admit to being wrong about a player's profile *because he believes all he can do is communicate correctly what he sees on film at that time in that player's career the rest is all up to that player.*

Well there you have it. I pull no punches even when profiling myself. Through this process of joining a draft site and doing profiles publically I have been at times vilified. I have been called the Rush Limbaugh and Simon Cowell of the draft world. I suppose calling me those names is meant as an insult but I took them as a complement because as much as you might dislike Rush or Simon everybody waits and holds their breaths until both those icons communicate their opinions about a political situation or a talented contestant. The reason for that "hold your breath anticipation" is because those two entertainers' opinions are considered above all to be honest. That's all anybody could ask for when evaluating talent, an honest opinion.

The End

About the Author

Drew Boylhart is a 1st time author. He has been interested in the NFL Draft since 1979 and has been writing public profiles since 2004. Drew is a New York State 1970 High School graduate, who did not discover that he is dyslectic until his late fifties and refuse to acknowledge it publically until the writing of this book. Drew believes that being dyslectic is more of an impediment then a disability. Drew believes, "The disability only comes from the inability to indentify it. Once it is identified it is no different than a left hand person living in a right handed world, you just have to learn to adjust and change the style of learning from the norm. The NFL draft did that for him and much more.